WHERE HEAVEN MEETS CHEYENNE

WHERE

HEAVEN

MEETS

CHEYENNE

AS IMAGINED BY:
CHARLES MACDUFF WESTERMAN

atmosphere press

© 2024 Charles MacDuff Westerman

Published by Atmosphere Press

Cover design by Ronaldo Alves

No part of this book may be reproduced without permission from the author except in brief quotations and in reviews. This is a work of fiction, and any resemblance to real places, persons, or events is entirely coincidental.

Atmospherepress.com

For Chuck, Dan, Lynn & Pam

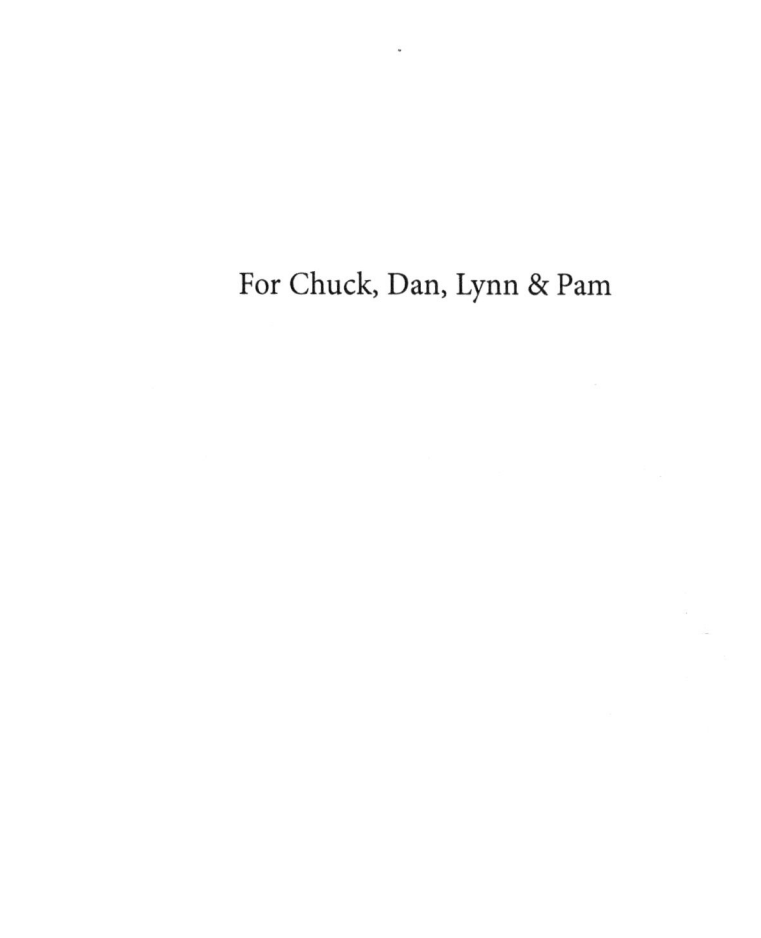

CHAPTER 1

Horses of Two Different Colors

**June 6, 1990–Chugwater, WY,
West Martellio Pasture**

Chuck Westerman rode his first horse on a cattle ranch in southeast Wyoming.

"Put your left foot in the stirrup there," Luke Bainbridge told Chuck, whose eyes had drifted to the old wooden barn by the corrals a stone's throw away, his thoughts drifting along with them as he imagined whatever weathered old cowboy had constructed it. One thing Chuck knew he'd never accomplish was building a barn with his own two hands. To the mild annoyance of his wife, he was about as useful with a hammer as a quadriplegic in a paddleboat. What he didn't know was that the weathered old cowboy who'd built the barn had—in a small but ultimately significant sliver of providence—actually been married to his mother's cousin, Tootie.

"Sorry. What was that?"

"Put your left foot in the stirrup."

"This thing, right?" Chuck said, pointing to the thing with a foot-shaped hole dangling from the saddle.

"Right as rain. You always mount on the left side cuz

that's how they've been trained. Make sure you've got a good hold on the horn when you put your foot in the stirrup—otherwise, you're skunked if your horse starts while you're trying to get on."

"I'm guessing that's the horn?" Chuck said, pointing to the thing sticking up at the front of the saddle.

"Dave said you were smart."

Dave was the pastor of Golden Hills Church in Cheyenne, the town where Chuck had shared the same occupation over the past four years. Dave also served as Chuck and Luke's mutual connection. A few weeks before, Chuck had casually told Dave he wanted to see *City Slickers* when it came to theaters at the Frontier Mall, which somehow ended up with Dave roping Chuck into accompanying him to Luke's ranch just outside the tiny town of Chugwater to help with a cattle drive of his own. Chuck was almost certain he wouldn't be any help, but was determined, at least, not to be any harm.

"Unfortunately for you Luke, I'm afraid being a Dartmouth man is useless when it comes to being a cowboy."

"We'll see if we can't make a cowboy out of you by the end of the day. Alright. Now—now put your foot in the left stirrup there—there you go—and now you're just gonna grab the horn with both hands—good—then just pull yourself up and swing your right leg over. Good, okay, now—put your right foot in the other stirrup, and you, my friend, are how they say, *mounted up*."

"Who exactly am I mounted up on?"

"Roy."

"Is Roy nice?"

"He's nicer than Biv."

"Who's Biv?"

"Biv is over there," Luke said, pointing to a restless-looking young stud with a coat like a sky full of stars. "I'll be riding Biv."

"That is much appreciated Luke. He's pretty though. What color of coat do you call that?"

"Blue."

"Huh…and Roy?"

"Roy is a bay horse. If I had to call his coat anything, I'd call it red."

"Alright, so where is the gas and brakes on ole Roy?"

Luke smiled in such a sympathetically amused way that Chuck swore he could read the two-word thought written in big block letters on his forehead, like the name of Billy Crystal's newest movie on a theater marquee—*City Slickers*.

"The gas is in your heels. Just give him a kick in the ribs and he'll start moving. You don't have to knock the wind out of him, but be firm and intentional so he knows what you want him to do. If you want him to go faster, just give him another kick, and he'll go into second gear."

"What's second gear?"

"Trotting."

"Third?"

"Loping."

"Fourth?"

"Galloping."

"How fast is galloping?"

"Fast enough you'll want to get off as much as you want to stay on."

"Got it. In that case, you better tell me where the brakes are."

"These are your brakes," Luke said, handing Chuck the reins. "…and your steering wheel. If you want him to stop, just pull back on the reins. Again, you don't have to choke him to death, but be firm so he knows you want him to stop. To turn him, all you have to do is pull the reins straight left or right. The steering you don't have to be as firm with—that can be more subtle. Just gently guide him. And make sure you've got an even amount of slack on each of the reins—otherwise, you'll think you're steering him straight, he'll think you want him to go left, and you'll both get frustrated."

"I'd like to avoid that."

"That's a good idea. They say a horse can sense two things in a man."

"And those entail?"

"Fear and anger."

"Huh…" Chuck said, trying to think of something to add to this simple but profound statement. As a pastor and an intellectual, he was typically wont to further conversation, but something in Luke's visage told him that, at this moment, there was more wisdom in the silence. His eyes drifted back to the barn. There was something about it. Some measure of charisma beyond physical appearance. The spirit emanating from the structure possessed an inexplicable yet undeniable holiness he was drawn toward. A small ethereal dose of what he imagined it would've been like to look into the eyes of Christ. The words came to him after a few moments, rather than him trying to come up with the words. "Fear and anger. That's good stuff Luke. Would make for a good sermon illustration somehow."

"Ya know, I've always thought that myself."

"Dave told me you're a good writer and have been known on occasion to fill-in at the pulpit for your church here in Chugwater and around Cheyenne a few times. He said whenever he hears you preach, he wishes he would've gone to work on a ranch instead of attending seminary."

"Well, I don't know about that," Luke chuckled. "If I had to crank one out every week like you, I'd need some formal training, but I suppose there's a few things you can learn out here you can't at a desk. I've got a lot of time to think about the nature of God, maybe even try to listen to Him every now and then. And yes, I enjoy writing. I suppose that's enough to make me good for three or four decent sermons a year."

"Suppose some week I experience a drought for sermon ideas. Would you mind if I dip from your well of fear and anger?"

"I'd be honored."

"You seem like an honorable man. I'll be sure to give credit where credit's due."

"What's on tap for this Sunday?"

"My sermon?"

"If you don't mind my asking."

"It's either a pastor's favorite question or the last one he wants to hear, depending on the week."

"Is this a good week?"

"I think so. I'm going to preach from Lamentations 3."

"If I remember correctly, that's the passage that inspired the famous hymn, 'Great Is Thy Faithfulness.' "

"Good memory. One of my favorite passages of scripture. Sometimes I read a passage and know I want to preach on it that week. But sometimes, I have to be patient, give my ideas time to sprout, grow, ripen. Let's just say I've been waiting to harvest this one for a while."

"Dave told me you're a pretty good writer yourself. You have a column in a magazine, right?" Chuck was no longer listening, his attention again raptured by the barn. The walls were a little out of line with the foundation. It was subtle, but there. Giving it a vulnerability that somehow made it more dignified than if it was standing perfectly upright. Like a sturdy cowboy who softens in his old age.

"What was that?" Chuck asked, peeling his eyes away from the barn.

"Dave said you have a column in a magazine."

"Oh, yes, *The Door*."

"Come again?"

"The magazine's called *The Wittenberg Door*."

"Ahhh."

Chuck wanted to change the subject, being as too many knocks on *The Door* in Wyoming opened the answer that it was considered one of—if not the only—liberal Christian magazine in the country. Luke seemed like a reasonable man, but so did Chuck's own father, until the two of them started talking politics from their respective (or, in this case, irrespective) sides of the dinner table. It was with good reason that five years ago, his mother had forbidden them to speak the words *Republican* or *Democrat* in her house.

"Why does that barn lean like that?" Chuck asked, both changing the topic and appeasing his curiosity.

"The wind almost always comes in from the west. Hence, its east-leaning posture."

"Only in Wyoming."

"That's right. No trees to stop the great unseen force of nature."

"Do you have a name for it?"

"My dad bought it from a man named Elmer Hersch. Hence, we call it the 'Hersch Barn.'"

"Huh."

"What?"

"For some reason, that name sounds familiar. I couldn't tell you why, but I swear I've heard it somewhere before. That must sound crazy."

Luke shrugged but maintained his silence as they both stared at Elmer Hersch's barn.

"Alright," Chuck said, giving Roy a couple friendly pats on his hulking right shoulder. "Now what?"

"Now, you're ready to ride off into the proverbial sunset."

"I'm not sure I am."

"No one's ready their first time—that's why there's nothing like it. That moment you feel more afraid than ever. That's when you know you're ready."

"Let's just hope it's not my last."

Luke chuckled softly and mounted up. The silence returned as they surveyed the prairie from their perches atop Roy and Biv. An ambling breeze rippled peacefully through the pasture grasses like a clean sheet being spread over a bed as a herd of antelope skirted west, Chuck's eyes following their lean white rumps through the valley across the whole of spring's palette—wildflowers speckling the prairie with Indian paintbrush, clover, aster, and elephant head. Notions of boldness flecked in their color. The treeless landscape hinted at vulnerability.

"Dave told me your wife has cancer." Chuck abruptly broke the silence.

"She does."

"How bad is it?"

"About as bad as it gets."

"I'm sorry to hear that. Dave says you and your wife are as good of people as he knows. My wife Diana and I have been praying for you and will continue to do so. Is there anything in particular we can pray for?"

"No more pain," Luke replied, a forceful tear leaking from his stolid blue eye.

Chuck wanted to ask for an explanation, but something inside him interceded. "Okay. No more pain. We can pray for that."

"Thank you, Chuck. You too seem like an honorable man. I hope you come back some day for another ride."

"Lord willing."

CHAPTER 2

As Far as the East from the West

August 25, 1973–Stevens Point, WI, Lake Joanis

This is the last one, Aaron Hamilton thought, his eager toes peaking over the ledge. It was the last day of summer. He had to make it count.

The hidden swimming hole at Lake Joanis—tucked away in a cove of archaic trees—was their favorite corner of the world that summer. A secret place, anonymous and shaded. A little heaven Aaron, Ty and the rest of the gang liked to frequent on sultry Midwest summer days.

The trees hiding the pool had been here long before anyone told them they were in Wisconsin. They were the kind of trees that could be trusted with secrets. All-knowing and no-telling, Aaron sometimes went to the swimming hole alone and told them things he'd never told anyone—how one day after his older sister Diana got done singing in church, their father informed her she sounded a little flat. How when he said this, Aaron watched Diana's face attempt to still the quivering lips and welling eyes, the sight of it causing Aaron to smile a smile he knew he shouldn't. He loved his sister, but she was too perfect, too grown up for her age. Even when she was little and he walked into her room, the floor was always spotless, the blouses always hung, the dolls always on the shelf. He was smarter, but she did her homework and got better grades. The trees kept his secrets, hiding them from the sun under a shaded canopy of woven branches and embroidered leaves.

#

Technically, it was the first day of school.

Resolved to be a better student than he'd been in Waukesha, Aaron was sitting at his desk five minutes before first period began, a personal record for him. But after an hour of listening to Mr. Kebbekiss deliver a pit-stained soliloquy on the horrors of gum-chewing, hat-wearing, and why it was important for a bunch of sixteen-year-olds to give a crap about Shakespeare, Aaron quickly remembered why he wanted to become a mechanic and never sit in a desk again. He looked down at his arms, long and athletic, then his legs, restless and idle, begging to be used.

As the hour wound down, Mr. Kebbekiss's spastic, dyslexic rendition of *Henry V's* St. Crispin's Day speech wasn't going over as well as it had in front of his bathroom mirror the night before. "By Jove, I am covetous for gold…wait," he said, giggling nervously, "that's not right…I am *not* covetous for gold."

Aaron sighed, his eyes drifting to the window. A cardinal stood proudly sunbathing on a nearby oak branch, bearing his vibrant red chest, mocking Aaron with freedom. Then, Aaron swore, the smug little bastard looked him square in the eye and winked. He winked! As if to say, "*You*, Aaron Hamilton, are a sucker." And that's when Aaron resolved there was nothing wrong with being a passable student and a prolific liver of life. It was hard to argue with fair weather, especially when days to sneak off to the swimming hole would be numbered till April. Soon, very soon, the snarling Midwest chill would arrive overnight. Like a ravenous Arctic wolf, it would sink its teeth in your keister and refuse to unclench its frigid jaw for six dark months.

He took out a piece of paper and scribbled a message to Ty, who was busy sketching a shockingly realistic and tasteful portrait of a topless Goldie Hawn. As Ty finished up the final, delicate touches on Goldie's right areola, Aaron discreetly placed a note in front of him which read—*Upon the tolling of the toiling bell, shall we leave hither, and hence doth slither, to the swimmering hole?*

Ty couldn't suspend a chuckle, and Mr. Kebbekiss, mistaking the chuckle as being jeeringly aimed his way, cleared his throat, mopped the sweat puddling on his brow with the back of his hand, and attempted to soldier on. "For he today that sheds his blood with me shall be my mother—brother!—be he ne'er so vile…"

Ty scrawled a brief reply and slipped the note back—*Doth not a bear crappeth in the woods?*

Mr. Kebbekiss glanced at the time winding down on first period and tried to quicken his pace. "This day shall gentle his condition; and gentlemen in England now in-bred—a-bed!—thall stink themselves accurs'd they were not here, and hold their manhoods cheap"—*RIIINNNNGGGG*—"whiles any speaks…"

Before Mr. Kebbekiss could say Saint Crispin's Day, they were in the parking lot halfway to Aaron's brown AMC Hornet, their hands almost on the door handle when a shrill, buzzkill of a voice called out, "Mr. Zielinski!" Ty rolled his eyes over his shoulder as Ms. Pressfield approached, then shaped his face in a saintly expression and turned to greet the assistant principal of Stevens Point High. "Ms. Pressfield! How are you? From the looks of you, it appears you had a very, very beautiful summer."

"Thank you Tyler. But you should know by now the more you flatter me, the more suspicious I get. Would you mind telling me where you and your friend here think you're going this fine morning?"

"That's a great question Ms. Pressfield. Great question. You see, I was just so excited to be back in school, I ran right out the door this morning without my backpack! This is my new friend, uh…Peter. He just moved to Stevens Point this summer, and he's such a good guy he offered to give me a lift home quick to grab it."

"Mmhmm…" Ms. Pressfield raised her thin, stringent eyebrows before narrowing them Aaron's way to take in the lanky, handsome boy with sandy blond hair tangling down over his ears standing before her. The rich brown eyes that took aim down a hooked, compact nose. "Peter who?"

"Humperdink, ma'am," Aaron answered. "Peter Humperdink."

"You don't live much more than a mile from here, do you Tyler?"

"About a mile and a half Ms. Pressfield."

"So you should be back in about…" She took note of the time on her watch. "Fifteen minutes then. Right?"

"Yes ma'am."

"Okay. Well, if somehow that doesn't happen, it would take more than a summer for me to forget your father's work number. Just food for thought," she said, then turned away and walked back inside. Aaron looked at Ty. "What now?"

"She's already gonna have her panties in a bunch when she realizes we gave her a fake name...and that the fake name we gave her was Peter Humperdink."

"I don't see why. Peter Humperdink is an excellent name."

"True, but I doubt she'll see it that reasonably, so we might as well get our trouble's worth."

They jumped in the Hornet. Rolled down the windows. Lit cigarettes. The penetrating voice of Mick Jagger crackling through the dusty speakers as Aaron cranked the volume pulling out of the lot and headed toward the lake. Trouble was later, freedom now. There was no Shakespeare or Ms. Pressfield or anything else they couldn't see right in front of them. At the moment, they were young. Their shoulders tanned and muscled. Their hair thick and breeze-blown. They were lousy singers, but no one could sing along to "Angie" like them. When "Angie" came on, they sang from the bottom of their souls at the top of their lungs.

"*Ayynn-jayyyy! A-yyyannn-jayyy! When will those clouds all disappear?*"

#

Initially, Aaron wasn't sure about the move from Waukesha to Stevens Point at the start of summer. He spent the first week cooped up in the house, missing his old friends in his old West Milwaukee suburb, ignoring his mother's request to unpack and symbolically admit they now lived in the quiet heart of the Badger State. Then his father—a paratrooper in Normandy—came home from work in a new car and his version of a good mood. He made spaghetti for dinner. The noodles buried under a wonder of red sauce, Italian sausage, mushrooms, zucchini, onions and black olives. It was

June sixth—D-Day. Mopping up the last of the sauce with a heel of garlic bread, Mac leaned back in his chair and dug the keys to the Hornet from the front pocket of his slacks. "Here," he said, tossing them across the table to Aaron. "I bought a new car today. The Hornet's yours."

"Thanks Dad," Aaron said, nodding *I love you*. Mac returned it with a quick wink, then commissioned him to take the Hornet and pick up Dilly Bars from the Dairy Queen for dessert.

"But come right back!" his mother called as he walked out the door. "It shouldn't take you more than a half hour."

There was a long line to the walkup window at the Dairy Queen, so Aaron parked and listened to the radio while the crowd died down. A group of kids his age were congregated on the outskirts of the lot, perched flippantly on hoods and tailgates, smoking cigarettes. He watched them for a while, deciphering the most approachable in the group. His eyes landed on a boy with brown, shag carpet hair and a friendly, perpetual smirk in his eyes. He smoked a cigarette in that languid, patient way of complete and mindful pleasure. Aaron stepped out of the Hornet, approaching him confidently. "Mind if I bum a smoke?"

"Not a problem my man!" Aaron took the cigarette and held out a firm hand to exchange names, then patiently waited for Ty to ask the next question as he lit the cigarette in the same languid manner and puffed away. "New in town?"

From that point on, Aaron had friends in Stevens Point. This is what the poor sap who ate lunch alone every day didn't get. Sitting at his private table, shoulders slouched, sheepishly hiding his face behind a book. Look lonely, and people will leave you alone. Aaron's trick was to act like he knew something they didn't. Like his own company was sufficient for him whether they joined him or not. Born with an unswerving belief in his abilities and a dry, charming humor, people got the feeling standing next to the tall, toned frame of Aaron Hamilton that the heights he would someday grow up to reach were limitless.

\#

The branch canopy covered all but the very center of the pool, which on cloudless afternoons was spotlighted with beams of sun so supernal even Aaron—who, unlike his sister, had never been much for church—couldn't fight the feeling something like God was near. He hadn't ruled out the possibility of God's existence, or even that He was loving in nature. If that God did exist, Aaron felt he had more of a pulse on His character than most of the shirt-tucking, finger-wagging WASPs he went to church with.

"Aaron! Get out of bed. We're leaving for church in ten minutes!" his mother had yelled every Sunday morning over the summer.

"Just because it's a building with a cross on top of it doesn't mean it's a church!" he retorted from under the covers. Not so much as a mild kickback of spiritual firepower had ever reverberated through Aaron's soul while sitting in the ass-numbing pews of their Midwestern, middle-class Congregational churches. Not in Waukesha. Not in Stevens Point. All the pastors ever did was get up in the pulpit and say what not to do…but those Sunday mornings when he and his father would beat the sun up to hunt—a huge aluminum thermos of thick-steaming coffee passing silently between them as they crouched, watched, listened—the chittering whispers of the early morning autumn woods, the fog peeling back off the land, a stately buck emerging from a thicket of trees to make his way across the open meadow, his father whispering, *You take this one*, the *click* of the safety and raising of Aaron's thirty-aught-six, the firm feeling of the stock in his shoulder, the front shoulder of his prey a step from the cross-hairs, a steady exhale and one eye pinched shut followed by another *click* with a simultaneous *BANG!...*

Pulsing through his veins those mornings was a communing delight with himself and his father, the buck and a sort of primitive Holy Spirit tribal cultures prayed to. He had this feeling as he watched Ty glide insouciantly through the liquid sunlight in the pool's center, and Aaron wondered if maybe that cardinal on the branch outside of class was God Himself—winking, giving him an omnipotent pass to skip school and enjoy friendship and creation.

"Throw me the rope," Aaron told Ty in his deep, Wisconsin bass of a voice that had deepened over the summer. "This is my last swing. My mother's gonna be mad enough without me missing dinner." He'd never met a person more spirited than Bea Hamilton. The fullness of her passion was one of the things he loved most about her, but that passion swung both ways. On a pendulum between jubilance and despondency, he watched his mother swing east to west and back again. She was the one who'd taught him to swim. When he was four and Diana was six, she took them to the pool at the Waukesha Country Club. Though he and Diana were adopted, both had, to a degree, seemed to curiously inherit their mother's natural ability in the water. And though Diana was a very capable swimmer, it was Aaron who was fearlessly dog-paddling about in the deep end at the close of the day. By the time he was twelve, his every movement in the water was executed with vigorous suavity.

"Oh Aaron, you swim so beautifully!" Bea would exclaim

when he performed the backstroke employing the magnificence of his swimmer's arms. Then he got old enough to want to swim alone with his friends, and she was at home worrying he'd drowned in the lake. She lent her passion so fully to his giftedness he sometimes wondered if she actually believed he put his pants on two legs at a time, then remembering his daring nature, worried he'd forgotten to zip them up.

"Here you go," Ty grunted, swinging Aaron the rope. "Don't hurt yourself now. Your face is already wrecked, but I'd hate for any harm to come to those delicate, feminine legs of yours."

"Tyler, your attempts to overcompensate for the fact I am ten-times more man than you'll ever be are nearly as amusing as they are pathetic."

"The day you're more of a man than me will be the day hell gets three feet of snow."

"Alright. Let's put a wager on it then. How much you wanna bet I can clear the far side of that patch of sunlight on this one?"

"A dollar."

The rope was tied to a branch that hung out over the water about fifteen feet from the ledge on the east side of the pool where Aaron was standing. The far western edge of the sunlit-patch stood about forty-feet away. For Aaron to clear it, he'd have to play the physics just right—using his arms to vault the rest of his body up and out, timing it at the very peak of his upswing in order to get enough leverage to clear the patch of sunlight.

"How about if I don't make it, I owe you five dollars, but if I *do*..." Aaron hesitated for a moment. "You let me ask your sister out."

By the look on Ty's face, Aaron could tell his friend was grappling with whether to be annoyed or amused by this. It was with a mix of both when he finally replied, "I thought you said she wasn't your type."

"C'mon dude. You know I like her."

"That's true. All my friends like Alicia. I was just hoping you'd keep pretending like you didn't."

"At least I tried, unlike your other friends."

"You know she's going to say no, right?"

This was probably true. Ty's stunning older sister was a near shoo-in to win homecoming queen for the senior class. She barely noticed Aaron the first few times he came to their house at the start of summer, thinking him just another one of her little brother's friends who gawked at her, which he did, but in a way more subtle and refined, more noble, than the rest who merely drooled over her rumored-to-be-perfect C-cups when Ty wasn't around. Would Aaron like to get his hands on them? Sure. What teenage boy in Stevens Point wouldn't?

More than that though, he wanted to kiss her svelte neck, to slowly work his lips over to her tawny shoulders. He wondered what it would be like for her to roll him over a little forcefully, to feel her firm, slender frame pressing into him, her bursting blue-green eyes looking only into his. How celestial to watch her take her long, fine brown-sugar hair down, the sweet smell of her strawberry shampoo washing over him. He'd made it a secret habit of opening the cap and taking long whiffs from the bottle whenever he went to the bathroom at the Zielinski's.

Ty was most likely right. Alicia would probably say no if he asked her out, but over the summer, there had been… moments. The first occurring one morning after Aaron stayed over at the Zielinski's. Around nine, Ty, as was typical, was a long way from getting out of bed. Other than Sundays trying to dodge church, Aaron had always liked mornings, especially in the summer. A little after seven, he headed down to the kitchen to see if there were any leftovers from Mr. and Mrs. Zielinski's morning pot of coffee. Both had left for work, and he was thrilled to find it still half full. Even more, he was thrilled to find Alicia sitting at the island counter, staring in quiet consternation out the window, holding a mug with both hands inches from her lips.

"Morning."

"Hey," she mumbled and took a drawn-out sip of coffee.

"You mind?" he said, nodding towards the pot.

"Go ahead."

He grabbed a mug from the cupboard, taking his time while he poured it. Relishing the savory, warming sound it made, plotting a way to breezily start conversation. When he turned back toward Alicia, she was still staring broodily out the window into the front yard, where two squirrels were engaged in a playful tussle.

"My money's on the one with the bushy tail."

"What?" She looked at him with a twisted face. A face that made him wish he'd have come up with a better, breezier opening line.

"Everything alright? You look like you're trying to break that window with your eyes."

"Oh," she said, smiling a little, "you're talking about the squirrels. Yeah, I'm fine, I guess."

"You guess?"

"I've just had better nights than last. That's all."

"Like how?"

"Like Greg and I got in a fight."

Aaron didn't really know Greg, but he'd been around him a few times, hanging out in the Dairy Queen parking lot, and had seen his band play at a couple house parties. Greg fancied himself the Mick Jagger of Wisconsin, but there was hardly anything special about him or his music. His voice was actually decent, his skills on the guitar adequate, but there was no substance in his lyrics, no soul in his melodies, no fire in his sound.

"I'd ask what it was about, but it doesn't really seem like you want to get into it."

"Sorry. I guess I just don't really know you all that well. I mean, you seem like a good enough guy. I know Ty really likes you. It's just, well, I had to stop being nice to his friends a long time ago, so don't take it personally. I wish I didn't have to come off as such a bitch, but if I don't, they get obsessed with me, and it's hard on Ty."

"I can see that. Lucky for us, I'm not obsessed with you, so if you want to tell me what's going on with that show pony you call your boyfriend, I'm all ears."

She laughed. A raspy, succulent laugh that made Aaron's head swoon.

"So if I walked over to you right now and tried to kiss you, you'd shoot me down?"

"Sorry," he said, shrugging his shoulders. "You're not my type."

"Really? Then what *is* your type."

"Girls who don't date show ponies."

"Okay, fine. Then riddle me this, *Aaron*—what would *you* do if there were rumors your boyfriend was fooling around on you, but he swore on his life he didn't?"

"Are we talking rumors or incriminating evidence?"

"I don't know. One of my friends is dating a guy from

Eau Claire who claims he saw him at a party after one of his shows dancing with some girl, then saw them leave together."

"What did Greg say?"

"He admitted to dancing with her. Said he was drunk, and it was a huge mistake, but swears on his band they didn't leave together."

"What do you think?"

"I don't know! That's why I'm asking you."

"Dump his ass."

"Just like that?"

"Yep."

"No second chances? No giving him the benefit of the doubt?"

"I'll give him one thing—he's a good liar."

"How do you mean?"

"He knows he doesn't have a chance trying to fib his way out of the part about dancing with her. Your friend's boyfriend saw it with his own eyes. There's more wiggle room on if they left together or not."

"You think they did?"

"I don't know Greg very well. I wasn't there, but what I do know about him and have heard of the story—yeah, I think they did. Even if they didn't, you really want to be with a guy who goes to another town, has a few drinks, and starts dancing with other girls?"

"What do you know about him?"

"I've been around him a bit. I'm good at reading people. Your brother's told me some things. He's not a big fan of him for what it's worth."

"Ty doesn't like anyone I date."

"Well, he especially doesn't like Greg."

"Fine. Then what's your read on him?"

"He dates you because it makes *him* feel good about *him*, not because he actually cares about you."

"Isn't that every guy?"

"Most. Not every."

"And you're not most guys?"

"Nope."

"And if I took the show pony to the glue factory, I'm guessing I'd suddenly be your type."

"I never said that."

"You're implying it then."

"I'm gonna hop in the shower," Aaron said, taking the last gulp from his mug and setting it gently in the sink. "See you around Alicia."

Her face twisted up again as he left the room. This time in a way that made Aaron want to break out dancing. She was unaccustomed to being the one walked out on, especially by a boy two years her junior. A few days later, he ran into her at the grocery store. She smiled as she walked up to him dressed in a pair of faded cutoff shorts, flip-flops and a painfully fitting peach-colored T-shirt. "Well if it isn't Mr. Not-Most-Guys."

"Miss Zielinski."

"Guess what?"

"You're a communist."

"No! I broke up with Greg."

"Good for you," he said, then let the silence hang.

"That's it?"

"What?"

"That's all you have to say, *good for you*? You're not going to ask me to go to a movie now or something?"

Of course he wanted too, but Aaron sensed he was being tested. Besides, if he ever did ask Alicia out, he needed to ask Ty first. Aaron owed him that for everything he'd done to welcome him to Stevens Point. "Nope. Like I said, you're not my type."

"I'm not dating the show pony anymore."

"Yeah, until you find the next one. Besides, even if you *were* my type, I couldn't do that to Ty."

"Good, because I'd have said no anyway."

"I'm guessing it's because *I'm* not *your* type."

"I didn't say that. Despite what you think, I've dated plenty of guys who weren't show ponies. I don't really have a type. You either catch my eye or you don't. For what it's worth, you're kind of cute when you try to act all confident around me. Doesn't matter anyway, though, because I don't date my little brother's friends."

"I don't try to act any way around you or any other girl. That's why I'm not most guys."

"I'll give you this—of all Ty's friends, I like you the most. Unfortunately, that still makes you my little brother's friend."

"So if I wasn't friends with Ty, you'd want to go to the movies?"

"I didn't say that." She smiled, then looked at her watch. "I should probably get home. Bye Aaron."

They'd run into each other a few times since then. At the Zielinskis', in the Dairy Queen parking lot. He didn't think it was a coincidence they always ended up having coffee in the kitchen together right after Ty's parents left for work when Aaron slept over. They hadn't broached the subject of dating since their exchange at the grocery store. Over time he learned she had good taste in music, a wonderfully sarcastic streak, and that she was so entirely disgusted by pickles she couldn't bear to have them anywhere near the vicinity of her dinner plate. Maybe she just liked the attention, knowing he wouldn't get too carried away with it. Maybe she'd bought his lie that she wasn't his type. Or maybe, just maybe, Alicia Zielinski, imminent valedictorian, unanimously voted the most beautiful girl at Stevens Point High according to the unofficial polls taken in the boys' locker room, maybe she was actually finding herself quite taken with Aaron Hamilton.

#

"Sorry man," Aaron told Ty. "I've got to at least try…c'mon! Who would you rather have dating your sister—me or another jerk like Greg Vetters?"

Ty pondered this for a while before saying, "Ten."

"What?"

"If you don't make it, you owe me ten dollars."

"And if she says yes, you won't be mad?"

"Deal's a deal."

Aaron had been looking for an opportunity to get Ty to give him a chance with Alicia. Now here he was—potentially forty feet from a date with her.

And so, Aaron Hamilton took his last swing.

CHAPTER 3

Fighting Cancer with Carrots

June 6, 1990—Chugwater, WY,
The Ranch House

Paige Bainbridge was lying in bed and eating a carrot.

"How'd it go?" she asked Luke with a smile, looking up from Flannery O'Connor's *A Good Man is Hard to Find*. He'd just come in from moving cattle to the summer pastures and could tell by her smile she was in a rare, sunny mood that these days were in sparse supply. At the moment, though, the weather was divine, and her morphine dosage had found that rare balance—sufficient to kill the pain without drowning her clarity.

"Oh, as usual, the cattle got a little riled up when it came time to push them through the gate, but we got them through without tearing up the fence and showed them where the mill was, so at least they know where to find water. If the wind doesn't pick up soon though, the mill will cease to be a place where water can be found."

"It'll pick up. I can feel it inside my bones."

Luke winced at the image—the place where all the darkness and decay of their lives resided. From the moment his high school sweetheart came out of the shower two years ago with a little towel wrapped around her head, a big one under her arms, and an expression fighting tears when she told him she'd found a lump, their lives had been marked by two distinctly separate eras—life *Before Cancer* and life *After Diagnosis*.

Life BC had consisted of growing up on the homestead ranch near the small town of Albin, an hour away from Chugwater. He'd been the star of the high school basketball team and state president of the Wyoming Future Farmers of America. At the age of twenty-one, he married the only girl he'd ever loved, Paige Alder, who also happened to be the Albin High head cheerleader and state president of the Wyoming Future Homemakers of America. They were the quintessential, small-town Wyoming love story. They were supposed to have a happy, peaceful, skin-wrinkled ending.

Then life AD happened and all that came with it—the tubes and morphine and throwing up. The crying and awkward conversations, weary prayers and constantly feeling oppressed by an imaginary dark cloud overhead following them everywhere and never feeling like they'd be able to run fast enough to get out from under it again…

The cancer started in her breasts, which the doctors were able to remove, but not before it had metastasized deep in her bones. She didn't have leukemia, a cancer of the cells that starts in the bone marrow. These cells eventually develop into functioning blood cells, which are then smuggled into the rest of the body. If not detected in time, this is how leukemia spreads to the organs and claims its prey. What Paige had was called secondary bone cancer. Meaning the cancerous criminals imprisoned in her marrow were some form of her original breast cancer cells. The body didn't ship these cells to the blood stream, which meant the cancer didn't spread to her organs, but remained trapped—gnawing at her skeletal structure without shutting down anything that kept her from staying alive. Effective battle strategies were being plotted in the worlds of both modern and holistic medicine at the time of Paige's diagnosis, but despite her voluminous hours of meticulous research, nothing to that point had been up to the job of evicting this darkness and decay from its dwelling place. Not chemotherapy or prayers on bended knees. Not the carrots she was eating by the bushel till her skin turned orange.

"Which one are you reading?"

"'Good Country People.'"

"Are you liking it?"

"Not particularly. The characters aren't very likable, but it's a good story, and it's well written. It makes me think about things worth thinking about, and that makes it worthwhile. I wouldn't say I particularly *like* reading the story of Job either, but that doesn't change the fact it's a good story. A reminder that I'm not God. That I'm not in control, and there are a great deal of things I don't know and never will. That my life and everything in it has been given to me by Him, and therefore He can allow it to be taken it away…"

They both fell silent.

In the two years since her diagnosis, this was the closest Paige had come to speaking of her death. Luke wasn't going to be the one to bring it up. Even if he wanted to, it wasn't his place. His place in all this was to be what his wife needed him to be. To be there to discuss every stratagem and resource at their disposal for overcoming her cancer, but not a word was to be spoken of what would happen if it defeated her. She had no time for that. Any minute spent preparing for the possibility of death was time she could spend fighting for her life. For two years, they had fought tooth, nail and bone marrow. Had traveled to specialized doctors in Spokane and Omaha. Fighting the fight. Hoping against hope. When nothing turned in the right direction after these visits, hoping they'd find hope again. After Omaha, they had their serious doubts, but last month Paige had discovered a specialized clinic in Bonn, Germany, offering trials for new and potentially groundbreaking treatments. They booked flights for August shortly thereafter. Since they'd bought their tickets, her good moods had been less sparse, her determination redoubled. The bag of carrots never out of reach.

Until they left for the clinic in Bonn, Luke knew his wife would eat twice her ninety-pound-body weight in carrots and spend as much time with the girls as she could. For every day she woke again was another day her daughters had an unconditionally loving and fully devoted mother in their lives. Every day she lived was another day she was there to teach them how to live as women of character.

"I had a very nice talk with Dave's pastor-friend, Chuck Westerman…" Luke finally said.

"Oh?"

"Very nice, interesting man. Grew up in Wisconsin, studied English at Dartmouth, moved to Chicago with his wife, where they helped run an inner-city ministry and tutoring program. Then a few years ago, he moved to Cheyenne to pastor Calgary Baptist."

"What made him go from inner-city ministry in Chicago to rural ministry in Cheyenne?"

"He just said he loved the West because he liked being able to see out. Then Cheyenne called, and he couldn't tell where it ended and Heaven began."

"Have you told him to check the Cheyenne Regional

Medical Center?" she jested, bringing up another painful image for Luke—the fateful diagnosis of his high school sweetheart in a colorless room with gray linoleum floors. "No, but he did say he'd pray for us, and asked if there was any specific aspect of our situation we needed prayer for."

"What did you tell him?"

He could tell her the truth—that he wasn't optimistic about Germany. That he'd asked the Reverend to pray specifically for no more pain, whether that be in the form of a miraculous healing or a more probable imminent death. He could tell her it felt like thorns were growing in his chest every time she winced and he couldn't do anything but increase her morphine drip. He could tell her no amount of carrots would ever hold a candle to terminal, bone-buried cancer, so she might as well stop turning herself orange trying to win a war they'd lost a year ago. That it was time to start reflecting on the life she'd lived, the time they still had together, and how he and the girls were going to go on living after she was gone.

What did she think about having Dana move into the basement to manage the house full-time? Did he have her blessing to remarry someday? How did she make that chicken tortilla casserole they all loved so much? Was it harder than tuna noodle bake? The last time he had to cook for himself was in his college days, where his highest level of culinary achievement had been the tuna noodle bake casserole. Once, during his freshman year of college, he'd made it on Christmas Break. They'd dated for two years in high school, but she'd broken it off the previous summer, citing distance as the reason, though Luke suspected, and later confirmed, the real reason—he wasn't a Christian. Then, on January 6, 1972, he called the Alder farm, and she answered on the third ring.

"Hello?"

"Hi Paige." It was the first time he'd heard her voice since the breakup.

"Luke! It's good to hear from you. How have you been?"

"Good. I've been good. How are you?"

"Great! It's good to hear from you…I already said that, didn't I?"

"You did."

They chuckled the kind of awkward, wincing chuckle of a past-intimate relationship attempting to make small talk. Luke soldiered through. "I guess I'll just cut to the chase—I've got some news. It's good news. Important news. The kind I'd rather tell you in person. Do you have plans tonight?"

"Not at all."

"Would you be interested in coming to the ranch for dinner? My folks are going to a rotary club meeting, so I'll be cooking."

"*You're* going to cook?"

"Yes."

"I don't believe it."

"Believe it lady! And not just some grilled cheese sandwiches and canned tomato soup! Tonight, I'm making my specialty."

"You have a specialty?"

"Tuna noodle bake casserole."

"Sounds fancy. What time?"

"Seven?"

"I'll be there."

At a quarter to seven, Luke saw the red truck appear at the top of the hill through the bay window in the kitchen, then slope down into the little creek-winding valley where the Bainbridge Ranch had successfully sustained three generations and counting, then rumble over the cattle-guard into the dirt driveway of his modest but dignified childhood home.

"You're early," Luke said as Paige came inside and took off her snow boots.

"By your standards, I'm right on time."

"That's true. Dinner's almost ready."

"I can smell that. I think this is the first time I've ever smelled seafood in this house."

"We're partial to beef."

Paige sat in the kitchen and watched him open a can of peaches while whistling "It Had to Be You." "You seem... different."

"Oh?"

"Not in a bad way. Just, I don't know, more joyful."

The timer dinged. He pulled the casserole out of the oven, triumphantly heaping a healthy scoop on her plate. "Here you go! T-N-B-C A LA L-U-K-E."

"Looks wonderful," she said, grabbing her fork to dig in.

"Wait!"

"What?"

"We haven't prayed yet."

"Prayed? But you don—"

Without saying more, he reached his left hand across the table and grabbed her right, bringing it to the center. With the warmth of a sheepskin blanket, he shrouded his other hand over the top of hers, then bowed his head. "Lord, thank you for this day. Thank you for a warm casserole on a cold night. For putting Paige in my life and all the ways she's shown me how deep your love runs." He framed his grip on her trembling hand. "And how that love played such a big part in the decision I made last night to give my life to following you. Amen."

He looked up across the table at the teary face smiling the most beautiful smile he'd ever seen. Perfectly capturing in a moment everything he loved about her. How her face scrunched at the corners as her mouth curved up, her crystal blue Swedish eyes retreating and transparent all at once, like the sun shining directly over two little glacial pools, its radiance penetrating deep as windmill wells. The thin, firm structure of her shimmering lips. The way they encapsulated her delicate beauty and quiet strength, and how they were on a collision course toward his own as he thought about all this.

#

"Luke?"

His eyes snapped from the distant memory to her face now—orange and twenty years older. The way it scrunched at the corners no longer emblematic of his winsome ideals but his wincing reality. "What did you ask Pastor Chuck to pray for?" she asked, then took a large bite off her carrot.

He hated that damn carrot almost as much as he loved it.

Everything he loved and respected about his wife was in the way she ate that carrot. Her small, strong jaw determined to beat cancer with carrots one bite at a time. How she was probably so sick of the taste of them that she hated carrots more than he did, but that hate was no match for her love—for the girls, for him, for all the people in their little Wyoming corner of the world. All this love that sprang from her well of love for Jesus. And she kept on choking those carrots down because she wanted to show people that hope wasn't wishful thinking but willful doing. That even if she died, carrots would still have beaten cancer. That her body may have been defeated, but her spirit hadn't wavered. In her very effort to live, she had shown him how to handle her death—one small, determined bite at a time, driven by a love that penetrated deeper than sorrow. And since she'd shown him this love all those years ago when he was nineteen, he would show it to her now. He wouldn't tell her to stop eating carrots. He'd go with her to Germany or Thailand or the bottom of the Mariana Trench if she asked him to. He wouldn't take away her hope, no matter how much it killed him to watch her fight for it.

"I asked Chuck to pray that God would have some good news for us in Germany." Then he kissed her in the same way she had all those years ago over a heaping plate of tuna casserole. As their lips collided, they were raptured for a moment back to the hope and joy of that night in the Bainbridge kitchen…how they'd kissed for what felt like twenty years and twenty seconds, then finally broke away and took up their forks to eat Luke's casserole. How when Paige took her first bite, a loud *crunch* reverberated from her jaw. "Oh!" she yelped, then spit the half-eaten bite out in her napkin. "Luke, did you, uh, did you *cook* the noodles before you put them in with the tuna?"

"No," Luke said, puzzled, thinking the noodles, like, *baked* when he put them in the oven. "Are you supposed to?"

"Oh Luke…" she said sweetly, then laughed as hard as she could ever remember. So hard that Luke started laughing at her laughing until both were laughing till they cried.

CHAPTER 4

The Bottom of the Mariana Trench

*June 10, 1990—Cheyenne WY,
The Parsonage*

Charlie was sleeping peacefully in his crib.

"Dye..." She stirred. "Dye?" She woke.

"Chuck?" Diana groaned, looking at the clock—the witching hour staring coldly back. "Chuck???"

Thud.

"Chuck! What's going on?"

It had come from the bathroom. He was in the bathroom. What was he doing making a raucous in the bathroom at three in the morning? First, he'd woken her up right after she'd drifted off, asking if she smelled something odd in the house. She didn't. He did. Odd. Then she'd finally got Charlie back down, and here Chuck was about to wake him up again. She opened the bathroom door, her eyes hating the light.

He was on the floor. Writhing. Drooling. Drool on his wispy mustache. His evergreen eyes rabid and electric, his gangly frame shaking like a broken motor.

#

It was early Sunday morning. Chuck had a good sermon prepared. Maybe his best. Lamentations 3:17-30. Jeremiah's been weeping for two and a half chapters as only Jeremiah can weep—*I have been deprived of peace; I have forgotten what prosperity is. So I say, 'My splendor is gone and all that I had hoped from the Lord.' I remember my affliction and wandering, the bitterness and the gall. I well remember them, and my soul is downcast within me...*

And just when the reader thinks Jeremiah couldn't be any more of a bummer, he hits them with this—*Yet this I call to mind, and therefore I have hope: because of the Lord's great love we are not consumed, for his compassions never fail. They are new every morning; great is your faithfulness. I say to myself, 'The Lord is my portion; therefore, I will wait for him.' The Lord is good to those whose hope is in him, to the one who seeks him; it is good to wait quietly for the salvation of the Lord. It is good for a man to bear the yoke while he is young. Let him sit alone in silence, for the Lord has laid it on him. Let him bury his face in the dust—there may yet be hope. Let him offer his cheek to one who would strike him and let him be filled with disgrace. For no one is cast off by the Lord forever. Though he brings grief, he will show compassion, so great is his unfailing love.*

So very, brokenly, beautiful.

The affliction, the wandering, the bitterness and the gall—then the hope, the compassions that never fail, the unfaltering love in the face of sorrow. The syntax, the phonetics, the imagery—perfectly capturing the gritty, glorious duel between despair and belief. Chuck felt he'd captured the beauty of this struggle in his sermon. That he and Jeremiah had collaborated to tell a story that would lead his flock to live more fully in the realities of love.

He would tell them of the time he and Diana lived in their tiny apartment in the heart of Logan Square, arguably Chicago's roughest neighborhood in the eighties. On Tuesdays, they'd eat their big meal out for the week at the burger joint down the street because Tuesday was two-for-one cheeseburgers. Saturday nights, they'd stay in, watch Eddie Murphy carry *Saturday Night Live* on their fourteen-inch rabbit-eared television while Chuck drank a couple Millers. Diana wearing his mother's hand-me-downs, his white Chuck Taylor's held together with shitty duct tape. "Yo Chuck!" kids from the Cabrini Green Public Housing Project would say. "Yo Chuck! You need new shoes, man!"

That was going to make the congregation laugh—these kids who fought through bitter Midwest Winters in worn-out hoodies and tattered denim jackets. Kids who ate off food stamps and kept away from windows in their own homes to avoid the angry bullets of poverty. It was these kids who were telling the grew-up-in-a-white-middle-class-family-and-graduated-with-honors-from-Dartmouth-director-of-the-inner-city-ministry that *he* needed new shoes. He and Diana smiled at this—if you're going to be poor, it's vital to develop a good sense of humor.

He'd pictured the members of his small Baptist church in Cheyenne finding the humor in it as well, then he'd pause and make his face serious again, prompting his congregation to lean in, listen harder, better—impatient for him to keep going. He'd tell them about the time he didn't lock the car. How he'd been in a hurry. Was just going to run up, change for his pickup basketball game at the Y, and come right back. Purposely didn't lock it. Didn't want to be that cynical, that untrusting of those he was trying to help. He got back in the car and looked down to find the stereo had been stolen—with it, the Bob Dylan tape in the cassette player. The one with "See That My Grave Is Kept Clean." That was his favorite.

Five minutes. He'd been gone five minutes.

He couldn't remember feeling so afflicted, so bitter, so gall—his so soul downcast. For the life of him, he couldn't find anything humorous about his poverty and the poverty around him in that moment. Usually, he would curse, but this, this was beyond cursing. This only made him weep. Then he heard a tap on the window, his favorite voice pronouncing his name. "Chuck?" His face was in his hands. "Chuck??" He looked up to see the strong, unmistakable hips of his wife in his mother's ash-gray jeans. He didn't know how to tell her. She'd been so faithful. Wearing the hand-me-downs. Never complaining he could only afford to take her out for two-for-one cheeseburgers.

She loved music. Loved to sing.

Would sing anywhere—showering, vacuuming, in the grocery store with dozens of people around. She'd sing as she drove past the Gangster Disciples—the infamous gang of South Chicago who controlled most of Cabrini-Green—belting out "Bridge Over Troubled Water" like she was driving down golden streets. Chuck noticed she tended to sing loudest when their checking account was lowest, as if her lungs were stoking the great fire in her chest, breathing new life into the places it was threatening to smolder out. His wife loved music, and he'd let them take the stereo. No. It wasn't the stereo being stolen he was upset about. It was everything the stereo being stolen represented—the afflicted of the world bringing affliction to their fellow humans who were trying to help them remember what prosperity felt like.

"Chuck!" He rolled down the window. "What's going on?" Diana asked, her face beaming with hope. He didn't know where to start.

"I went up to…they took the…" Shit. He couldn't tell her the despairing news with that hopeful look on her face. "Why are you smiling like that?

"Get out of the car."

He slowly did as he was told. She grabbed him by the waist, pulling her hips to his. "I'm pregnant."

They named him Jeremy. Jeremiah wasn't endearing enough for Dye, but Jeremy she loved. When he came out late in May 1983, not crying but sucking his thumb, Chuck knew he'd be strong like his mother. Knew it from the way he held his chest out. His shoulders were a little small, but his chest was broad and proud. His head had a way of resting slightly tilted down—not out of fear–but because his eyes were interested in what lay ahead rather than above, as if preferring the marvel of trees over stars. He had some of his father's brains, but more of his mother's heart. Her beautiful, resilient, Armenian heart beat in his firstborn's chest like rocks on love's window.

And in that moment his wife told Chuck his story was going to live on, that he could die tomorrow and still be living, that their love had produced a legacy that would wake each morning and carry out the testimony of their love. That in his love's womb was the evidence of love's resilience. Of all the love that had been made to overcome the unlovely and produce this miracle. He and Diana had made love, his parents had made love, her parents—whoever they were—had made love. This miracle that wouldn't have been possible without two Armenian kids who mistook passion for love but at least loved their mistake enough to realize they weren't prepared to give her the love she needed and gave her to someone who would.

It was at this moment the Reverend understood the beauty of Lamentations.

How the fibers of death and sorrow had provided the nutrients for life and hope—this tree of life that would be his son—to grow. And as long as there was light, every morning being reborn, it could renew, transform, photosynthesize, death into life. And even when evil tried to make him think the music had been stolen forever, when he felt deprived of peace and had forgotten what prosperity felt like—God's mysterious and unfailing love had offered to be his portion—had offered his cheek to take the blow, Himself to be filled with disgrace.

"When I read words like the ones in Lamentations 3," Chuck had planned to preach, "words that speak to the very core of my soul, I always try to picture who was writing it. Where they were writing it. When they were writing it. Like how did Jeremiah go from Hell to Heaven so quickly?

"As Christians, when we read the Word, we tend to forget that someone, somewhere, in some time, actually had to sit down and write these words. And it was just as quiet and frustrating and mundane as it is when I sit down to write. Jeremiah couldn't be certain his words would transcend time, foreshadow the life of the savior of the world. Only God knew that. Jeremiah himself only knew what he thought and felt in the moments he was writing it. And something, something ordinary yet profound must've happened between, *my soul is downcast within me*, and, *yet this I call to mind, and therefore I have hope...*

"See I think he'd been up all night, unable to sleep.

Wracked with the fear of himself—of being powerless to sin and death. That by his own power, he had no control over, was no match for, evil. And he'd been writing about this waking nightmare all night. Two and a half chapters of darkness and despair and the idiot, *we* idiots, always forget the very important fact that God has never once failed to make the sun rise.

"It'd been one of those nights for Jeremiah. Those nights when you're sure—*this is the night it's never going to come up again*. And after he'd written *my soul is downcast within me*, he realized he'd found the spiritual bottom of the Mariana Trench, the absolute lowest point on Earth, and his perception of the world's circumstances made him weep enough tears to fill seven seas.

"This perception had become his reality. His belief that the sun would never rise again had brought him to a place where he was surrounded by darkness—crushed by the weight of the very seas he'd wept. And this thought was so terrible he put his face in his hands and wept some more.

"Then something beautiful, that for me had strong hips and ash-colored jeans, called his name. 'Jeremiah! Get out of the car! Get up and look at me!'

"And tearing his face from his hands, he looked up, and there, shining through the window, was the rising sun—the great, unfailing faithfulness of God. And as the corner of his newly born smile caught the last tear streaming down his cheek, Jeremiah picked up the pages that had already been written, but he didn't tear them apart. He didn't try to pretend this story of his pain didn't happen. Didn't try to pretend he was a man incapable of being incapable. No. He left those pages as they were. He wouldn't go back and change the story he had written. He would only change the story he had yet to write. And with the radiance of a new sun and a smile on his face, he picked up his pen and scribbled the words that contain the very essence of salvation—*yet this I call to mind, and therefore I have hope…*"

Certainly, it would've been the best sermon Chuck Westerman ever gave. The perfect blend of laughter and tears. Souls would've been swayed, swooned, saved. But he never did give it. The seizure he was having on the bathroom floor erased any memory of ever having written it.

CHAPTER 5

A Halo Made of Steel

March 13, 1974—somewhere over the Rocky Mountains

Aaron would miss the mountains.

He'd miss the staff at Craig Spinal Cord and Brain Injury Rehabilitation Hospital too, but more in that way Vince Lombardi's players missed their tough old coach—remembering him fondly yet not exactly pining to be back with him on the practice field. For all the money in the world, Aaron wouldn't go back and relive the past six months, but he'd live the rest of his days knowing that a boy wouldn't have survived what he had since that fateful day in August. Had it only been six months? It felt like twenty years since the branch holding the rope snapped and he plummeted headfirst on a rock in the shallows of the pool.

Such is time.

As the plane carried him away from the Rockies, sights set on Wisconsin, he contemplated, step by gritty step, the daily mountains he'd climbed since Ty rescued him from the bottom of Lake Joanis.

When he got to the E.R., they transferred him onto a specialized gurney, then rolled him over facedown. The platform of the gurney ended at his chin, with a little ledge extending out about a foot below it. On this ledge was a stainless-steel pan, which Aaron could make out his vague reflection in. Before they started shaving, the nurses asked if Aaron preferred his hair just be taken off on the sides or if they should buzz the whole thing. He opted against the mullet. When they started drilling pilot holes to put thumb screws in his skull right above his ears, no such consultation was had. Since it was a neck injury, morphine and other painkillers were forbidden as they stole oxygen the spinal cord eminently needed to minimize the damage of his injury. Instead, they injected each side of Aaron's skull with Novocaine where the screws would go in, then set out drilling the pilot holes in the semi-numbed area. This was done with your basic crank hand drill. The sound it made was ungodly, and the word to describe the pain doesn't exist in this world. Shortly after they started drilling, Aaron felt something warm trickling down from head to cheek, then saw a crimson bead dropping into the pan below…*splat*.

As they drilled and screwed, drilled and screwed, the process repeated itself. *Drip* and *splat*, *drip* and *splat*. Drip by drip, drop by drop, the blood slowly pooled in the steel pan. By the time they secured what looked like a set of large, blunt, stainless steel ice tongs arching over the back of his head to the screws, he could no longer make out his reflection in the murky red pan—the blood running down his face like Christ's with a crown of thorns.

They transferred him again, this time to a specialized bed, again facedown. Once in place, they fastened a rope to the ice tongs. The rope was on a pulley, the other end tied to what looked like a meat scale—a round, cylindrical bowl holding a forty-pound weight to buoy Aaron's neck, and for almost two weeks, his view was nothing but a white-tiled floor.

At last, a nurse came in and said they were taking him to the O.R. to put him in a steel halo body cast. *Halo* sounded a lot more pleasant to Aaron than *ice tongs,* so he thought maybe things were looking up.

They were not.

Next thing he knew, they were wheeling him down to the O.R., where they parked him under two of those big, hot, blinding lights they have in such rooms. Before they even started removing the thumb screws, he was drenched in sweat. They took out the screws, shaved his head again, and Aaron thought, *oh shit.* Then he saw them filling a syringe with Novocaine again, and he thought, *shit, shit, shit!* This time they injected him with four shots in each corner of his skull. Then they showed him the halo—a beautiful ring of stainless steel—sized it up proportionally to his head, and grabbed a screwdriver. A flathead. Just like the one in the utility drawer of the Hamiltons' kitchen. Aaron would never forget that screwdriver. A devil-red handle with a steel shaft forged in the ninth circle by the dark prince himself. The nurses held him still while the doctor took four icepick-sharp screws and started cranking them in. They were about the same thickness as the thumb screws, but four of them this time. The threads of the screws twisting in the corners of his skull sounded and felt even worse than the drill bit. Again, the precise single word to describe it doesn't yet exist, but to try and put it into a somewhat clear and brutally vivid description, at the time it was happening, he would've told you he could hear the skin and muscle and bone that encapsulated his consciousness in this world popping and snapping and crunching twice as clearly. Each screw put about ten pounds of pressure on his skull. He thought his eyes were going to pop out of his sockets after twenty.

Fastened to the ceiling above his bed was another pulley. This one with hooks fastened to the rope ends, looking disturbingly like the kind of pulley found in a packing house. The halo secured around his head at last, they wheeled him to a different recovery room where they brought in a metal cart and set the brakes at the foot of his bed. Then they fixed one of the hooks on the rope end to the front of the halo and, using the pulley, raised him upright thirty degrees—the first time he'd sat up in two weeks. Hooking the other end to the metal cart to anchor him, Aaron remembered looking at his toes, then blacking out.

The smell of salts brought him back into the world of that room. An angel of a nurse dabbed his forehead with a cold cloth. From the sides of the halo, two bolts stuck out like those in the neck of Frankenstein's monster. They propped him up more until he was ninety degrees, re-anchored the pulley, and attached two metal uprights to the Frankenstein bolts, the uprights running down over the top of his shoulders. Once in place, they put a cloth vest on him, then built a huge cast around the vest and the uprights.

Up to this point, Aaron hadn't been informed of the nature of his injury. He'd figured out something was seriously wrong with his neck, but hadn't asked, because, *frankly*, he was afraid to hear the answer. His family had been told he was paralyzed, but to what degree of permanence and severity, they weren't sure.

"It's a cervical 5-6 spinal injury," Dr. Frank Magnuson told the Hamiltons the next day as he touched a long, bony thumb to his nose.

"What does that mean?" Diana asked.

"The injury occurred in the fifth and sixth vertebrae, which means it's permanent and he's never going to walk again."

"Oh Aaron!" Bea cried, throwing her arms around her stone-faced son.

"I'm sorry," Dr. Magnuson said unconvincingly, then continued his plowing through the conversation. "But he'll be lucky to live to twenty-six, and the chances of getting to thirty are slim to none."

"What makes you say that?" Aaron asked.

"Because a stage C-5-6 injury qualifies you as a quadriplegic, not a para," Dr. Magnuson replied with a furrowed brow and what looked to Aaron like a smile in the shallow lines of his forehead. "Albeit you're an incomplete quad, which means there's still mobility in your arms and some in your hands, but your dexterity is only semi-functional. To be completely frank, it doesn't really matter if you're a complete or incomplete quad. I've never seen any of them make it past twenty-six."

The room was silent for a long time until finally, Aaron asked, "So if you're completely Frank, does that mean there's also incomplete Franks? And if so, how long do you give *them* before they kick the bucket?"

"Clever." Dr. Magnuson laughed wryly and looked at his watch. It was 5:13. His shift should've been over thirteen minutes ago. "Well, I'm sorry I didn't come with better news, but I need to go check on some other patients." He finished and began to leave the room.

"Before you go Doc, is there any way I can get your home address?" Aaron asked.

"Home address?" Dr. Magnuson frowned. "Why?"

"Because I want to forward you all the cards I get on my thirtieth birthday."

#

Ty came the next day—the first time they'd seen each other since the accident, as so far only family had been permitted to visit—accompanied by Alicia.

"I owe you ten dollars."

"Bets off on account of a faulty tree branch…" Ty quipped back in a shaky voice.

So far, throughout the whole ordeal, Aaron had sealed his emotions in an airtight container and buried it deep down inside himself. He hadn't cried or outwardly raged against his misfortune, instead electing to adopt a more subdued, cynical demeanor. But Dr. Magnuson's recent, permanent, permeating news and the sight of Ty and Alicia—the friend who'd welcomed him to Stevens Point and saved his life, the only girl he'd ever thought he loved and now felt he never could—stirred up a sudden flurry of emotions. He was doing a pretty good job keeping the lid on them in this moment of thorny silence until Ty finally broke it. "I'm sorry man," he said, tears rupturing out of him. "I'm so sorry. It was so stupid. We should've just stayed at school."

This thought had tortured Aaron many times over the past weeks, and he knew that, in a way, it would for the rest of his life, but he also knew Ty had been agonizing over it too—blaming himself for what happened.

"It was an accident Ty," he said, his own tears leaking reluctantly out. "It was *my* idea to skip class. It was *my* idea to make that bet. All you—" He had to pause there, the words in his throat momentarily suspended as a massive wave of despair and affection crashed over him. "All you did was save my life."

Alicia grabbed Aaron's hand, squeezing it with delicacy

and strength. Ty wiped his face with the back of his wrist and managed to get out, "Can I tell you something?"

"What?"

"Your mom called my parents and told them what the doctor said yesterday. If it was me in your bed right now and you were the one standing where I am, I'd bet he was probably right. But you're going to make it through this man. You're stronger than me. You're stronger than anyone I've ever met. If anyone can do this, it's you."

"Thanks dude."

"No sweat," he said, glancing at Alicia. "I'll let you two talk. My parents said to tell you they're praying for you. I'll be back soon, alright?"

"Alright."

Alicia was still squeezing his hand as Ty left the room and closed the door.

"How are you doing?" she asked in that raspy, honey voice. And he couldn't hold it in any longer. The thing he'd been wanting to tell someone ever since the accident. That he hadn't been able to tell his parents or sister or best friend. To his dismay and relief, it burst out of him. "I'm terrified Alicia. I've never been so scared. I don't see how this turns out okay for me."

She squeezed his hand tighter, and he wanted to die at the realization that what he most wanted was to be held by her, but as he was buried under two inches of plaster, his head set still as a fencepost in the halo, he couldn't.

"Hey...Hey. Ty is right. *You* were right. You're not most guys. You're stronger than most. There's something sterling about you, Aaron Hamilton, that's very special," she said, then added, "I wouldn't be attracted to you if that wasn't the case."

The words penetrated his cast and embraced him, a big charge of elation surging through his tears with a hearty laugh. "I knew it!"

"You sound pretty excited for a guy who just got told that by a girl who isn't his type."

"Seeing as I now can't dance or hold the door open, I might have to lower my standards."

"I'm flattered. So? What's next?"

"I'll be right in this exact spot for the next six weeks. Then they're flying me to some rehab clinic in Denver for a while."

"Well, hang in there, okay? I should probably go. Ty's waiting for me, but, um, do you like to read?"

"Not really."

"What if *I* was reading to you?"

"I suppose I wouldn't hate it."

"Maybe I'll come in with a book one of these days and we can try it out."

"Okay."

"Bye Aaron," she said, bowing her head and kissing the back of his hand.

For six weeks, Aaron idled in the steel halo cast, Dr. Magnuson's skeptical prediction orbiting daily through his mind. Alicia came by two or three times a week to talk and read him *East of Eden*. He found it ironic he related to the swarthy character of Cal more than the golden-haired, halo-headed Aaron. She could've read him Leviticus and he would've been perfectly happy just listening to the undulations of her seraphim voice.

Ty visited him most days, keeping him up to date with the latest news at school, sometimes bringing him a new cassette for his tape player; *Moondog Manitee* (The Band),

Desperado (the Eagles), *Pronounced 'Lĕh-'nérd 'Skin-'nérd* (Lynyrd Skynyrd).

Other friends came. Signed his cast. Tried to be sorry, funny, make it better. Mostly they failed, but the effort was there and therefore appreciated, so maybe, in a way, they'd succeeded.

#

On the plane back from Denver, Aaron realized he owed Dr. Magnuson a small debt of gratitude for telling him, albeit tactlessly, the unabashed truth. Complete or incomplete, quadriplegics in 1973 didn't stick around too long. Had that fact been sugar-coated, he might have approached his rehab with less fervor, which would've been an unaffordable mistake. The fire the skeptical Dr. Magnuson had lit under Aaron's chair-bound keister stoked his resolve through trying moments of rebellious, derelict temptation. In four months of rehab, Aaron's only act of defiance had occurred on the plane ride to Denver.

His mother had been his accomplice.

Fifteen minutes from landing, Bea stirred him from a nap to inform him they were getting close. He'd shed the steel halo body cast a couple days before, but still had to fly on a backboard with a neck brace. Sunlight glistened through the window, kissing his cheek. Lying on his back, he strained to see out his peripheral, but his field of vision was limited to the interior of the plane.

"Can you see the mountains?" he asked Bea.

"Yes. They're beautiful. Can you?"

"No."

She looked around to see if any of the orderlies were

watching. After confirming a clear coast, she unbuckled her seatbelt and carefully rolled Aaron over on his side, enabling him to lay his eyes on the Rocky Mountains for the very first time. One look and he loved them forever. They were kindred spirits, Aaron and the Rockies. Young, tall and rigid. Their posture emanating an unmoving courage. And before the orderlies had a chance to scold Bea and roll Aaron back over, the mountains told him Frank Magnuson would only be proven wrong if he was obedient and courageous in the months ahead.

His first day at Craig, he found the staff to be friendly but stern. The first thing they told him was the extreme importance that he listened and did *exactly* what they said. They didn't water down the fact they were going to ride him like Secretariat, but promised it would always be for his ultimate well-being. There was a realistic yet hopeful authenticity in their approach Aaron responded to with full devotion.

Boy did they ride him though.

Sometimes pleasant and encouraging as they did, sometimes being stern and unforgiving about it. At Craig Hospital in 1973, going to therapy wasn't optional. Aaron didn't get to choose if he wanted an electric wheelchair or a manual. Rehab for an electric was less labor initially, but the more active and independent a quad he became—the nurses assured him—the more his quality and quantity of life would increase. Bring on the manual! He approached every physical therapy exercise as if it were life or death because, well, it kind of was.

Of course, there were days he was tempted to half-ass it. Try to trick the staff into believing he couldn't carry his cross another step when he knew there was still another mile in him somewhere. Every time he wanted to do the comfortable thing, he felt the mountains staring at him through the window, whispering a mantra—*If you sit, you die. If you sit, you die. If you sit, you die.*

He would sit for the rest of his life, but a manual chair required a much more active kind of it than the stagnating nature of an electric. Before long, he was transferring from bed to chair and back with impressive proficiency. By his last week at Craig, he was wheeling himself all over the facility by the strength of his own two arms.

As the plane ascended over the Rockies, Aaron reveled in all he'd overcome since the first day of school—resurrecting from the bottom of Lake Joanis and summiting a mountain few ever could. Then, climbing above the clouds, the mountains disappearing below, plane and glory leveled off, until eventually, they descended on Wisconsin, bringing down with them an unsettling and trepidatious question—now what?

CHAPTER 6

The Day the Stones Stopped Rolling

June 13, 1990—Cheyenne WY, somewhere between CRMC and The Parsonage

Chuck didn't have epilepsy.

He had cancer. A tumor in his brain the size of a pea.

"I'm a pea brain," he joked as Diana drove them back to the parsonage from Cheyenne Regional Medical Center. The last time they'd been there was three months before, the day Charlie was born.

"Chuck..." Diana sighed.

"What?"

"Just, not now."

"You know we're going to have to make stupid jokes if we're going to get through this."

She thought about it. It certainly was ironic. Her husband—the English major who graduated from Dartmouth with honors. He'd gotten in because he had a 4.0 GPA and an ACT score of 33. She'd stopped playing Boggle with him three years earlier for two reasons. The first being he had a dictionary on the inside of his eyelids. The second was that when he competed, he had the tendency to act like a gloating dickhead. The last time they'd played, he'd been such a gloating dickhead she ended up throwing the little wooden letters at his face and storming out.

"After your operation, we should play Boggle again."

"You know, it's insensitive to make fun of people with cancer."

#

It was funny, Chuck thought, them sticking it to cancer by laughing at it. They wouldn't give his tumor the dignity of admitting their fear. No. They'd eat whole cloves of garlic and laugh in its face. Would put on a red nose and oversized shoes. Paint big, fake smiles on their face and laugh, then laugh at it some more. The only problem was their second-born son Mick was terrified of clowns. But they had to find some way to keep laughing. Find some way to cope with reality and call hope to mind.

The Stones stopped rolling as the A-side ran out on the cassette. Chuck pushed the eject button and flipped it over. "Time Is on My Side" lurching slowly into motion like a tired steam engine. He couldn't die. He had to be around to teach Mick about Jagger and why clowns and cancer were nothing to fear. Mick had come bowling into the world in September of '86 after they'd left Logan Square and moved to Ukrainian Village. His head was flat-backed, and his two greatest talents were sleeping and running into things. His block-shaped skull rammed into things with such frequent and sadistic force Chuck had jestingly christened him Old Wooden Head, or Woody for short. Yet there was a grace about Woody and his violent crashing into things, like he was born for impact. Welcomed it. As if the impact was more afraid of him than he was of it. His full name was Mitchell. The last name of Diana's grandparents on her mother's side. They both liked *Mitchell* but hated *Mitch*.

"We could call him Mick."

"Mick? Like Mick Jagger?" Diana said skeptically. But Chuck was a Westerman and, like all good Westermans, had a gift for persuasion. A gift he spent the next hour using until Diana came around on the idea. Of his three sons, Mick came out the biggest. His shoulders so broad and such a weight to hold up he had a tendency of letting them slouch. When he stood up straight, Chuck recognized those shoulders as the almost exact replicas of his Uncle Son. Son, Chuck's uncle on his mother's side, had played on the same team as Willie Mays in the minor leagues.

And so Chuck knew his second son was born with great potential. That whatever he chose to run into, he'd run into with great force. He also knew this potential would always be competing with his want to sleep, to slouch through life. He got more of Chuck's brains but less of his mother's heart, and even though life would come easier to Mick than it would for Jeremy, he'd have less drive to fulfill it.

No. Chuck could not, must not, would refuse to, die. If God himself tried to roll the stone over his tomb, he'd stop it.

He had to be around to teach Woody about the illogical fear of clowns and the wonder of Jagger, to remind him not to slouch, to stand up straight—that the fate of all his secondborn's battles would be decided in the war of his posture.

"We're gonna get through this," Chuck told Diana as they turned down the street where the parsonage rested. Pulling into the driveway, the B-side made the sound of being eaten as the stereo malfunctioned and started chewing up the tape.

Ti-i-ah-i-i-ime is on my—

CHAPTER 7

The City of Cab Drivers with PhDs

January 6, 1979—Boston, MA

Apart from the seafood, things in Boston hadn't turned out like Diana had hoped.

In New England, her freshly notarized psychology degree from Trinity Baptist College only qualified her for more school or jobs that couldn't pay rent anywhere worth living in Boston. Between the nearby Ivy League schools, the small private colonial colleges that might as well be Ivy League schools, and the romance that occurs between Boston and every twenty-something who went to school or lived there for a summer—Diana was finding the problem with trying to live in a decent neighborhood in Boston was that a lot of other people were trying to do the same thing. People with more ostentatious educations and, therefore, the leg up to get jobs that paid rent in those neighborhoods. Even then, a Harvard education didn't guarantee you a decent-paying job with a career trajectory and a modest studio in Dorchester. On a rare occasion when Diana had sprung for a cab in the city, one of her taxi drivers had used that word, *ostentatious*.

Welcome to the city of cab drivers with PhDs.

Sometimes Diana wondered if she'd been living the same day since she'd come to Boston in September and walked up the front steps to Aunt Gladys' and Uncle Herman's beautiful Victorian brownstone in Back Bay. Never much of a morning person in college, Diana found she enjoyed rising with the sun on the East Coast. The day's obstacles felt small and manageable compared to the motivation that filled her spirit each morning at the thought of being one of America's first to rise. At seven-fifteen, she boarded the T with a thermos full of extra-hot black coffee, a big purse slung over her shoulder and an optimistic smile. She had a car—the Hornet—but unless she was driving to her Aunt and Uncle's church or making the two-hour drive to see Chuck at Dartmouth in Hanover, she preferred getting around Boston via the T. Milwaukee and Chicago weren't exactly tea parties to drive in, but navigating the maze of brick one-ways and back-alley boulevards in Boston was a massacre on her nerves, sense of direction and, most likely, her insurance premium.

The beginning of 1979 welcomed New England with a warm January. On the third, it even peaked above sixty for a few hours. That week, around noon Diana could be found masticating her pen cap, sitting on a bench somewhere in the greater Boston area, soaking up as many ultra-violets as she could while scouring *The Globe* classifieds or a map of the greater Boston area. She preferred masticating gum, but the rent prices in the neighborhoods she was aiming for were enough to make her swear off Wrigley's.

January was always the hardest for Diana.

The holiday hangover, the ominous, long stretch of dark and chill, and still a month away from finding out if that damn mythical groundhog would get spooked by his own damn shadow or not. So, she sat there on the park benches against all odds, trying to make life in Boston happen. Tapping her pen on her leg in staccatos, biting down anxiously on the cap, straining to see the colorful world she started the day with as her perceptions of life after college met reality in a clash of black and white scouring through the classifieds. At five o'clock, she was on her way back to her aunt and uncle's from whatever unsuccessful apartment hunt or job interview she'd failed to turn into gainful employment.

By January sixth, the sun dying over the western horizon far too early, her spirits and savings were growing malnourished. Like a snake returning to its den after an empty hunt, Diana sat digesting the reserves of her optimism in the steel belly of the T as it slithered across the Charles River on the orange line, making its way to North Station, where she'd jump the green line to Back Bay. Rummaging through her spacious purse, she pulled out a list titled *Good Neighborhoods to Live in Boston* and drew a line through ~~Thompson Square~~ and ~~Bunker Hill~~, joining the rest of the crossed-out names on the list she and Chuck had come up with back in August. From her crowded seat on the T, Diana fought back tears as she watched the sun die over America like her hopes of being close to her fiancé while he finished his last semester at Dartmouth. It had seemed like such a perfect plan. Boston being only a 120-mile drive from Hanover, she'd dreamt of living in New England after college ever since the first time she went to visit her cousins at their summer home on Nantucket.

Those were the days. Legs dangling on the porch swing overlooking the harbor at sundown. Guzzling down clams in droves. Mopping up melted butter with fall-off-the-shell lobster. Oysters on the half shell. Broiled bluefish. Thick-cut swordfish steaks searing on the grill. Marinated in a base of white wine, olive oil, lemon juice, soy sauce and garlic... the memories seemed tainted now by the last four months. Like the nostalgia of her youth had snared her in a net of post-college ignorance. You couldn't get seafood like that in the Heartland. By the time it got to Wisconsin, it had been dead too long. Apart from Chuck, her choosing Boston over Milwaukee was naively based on the quality of the shrimp cocktail, not the actuality of being able to afford a lease. The thought of faking optimism and hiding embarrassment in front of Aunt Gladys again was more than she could bear to think about, and her urge to prove she was a capable adult wouldn't allow Diana to break down in front of her.

Alright, Lord... Diana prayed silently. *I really don't know what I'm supposed to do right now, so you're gonna have to figure something out.*

As the T pulled into North Station, the window she was looking dejectedly out of stopped next to a poster with the word *Dunkin'* spelled in dull construction orange over the flat hot pink word *Donuts*, and her mouth was consumed by a hankering for bitter and sweet. She would've bet the entire contents of her twenty-five-pound purse the success of Dunkin' Donuts owed just as much—if not more—to the pairing of these colors than any donut recipe. The sage, practical working man's orange invoking imagery of hot coffee in foamy cups, a day of hard-fought productivity. The energy and creativity in the child's-play pink eliciting chocolate frosting and rainbow sprinkles. The whole appeal of coffee and a donut expressed in the two colors used to spell the name.

At this point, the replenishment of her spirits was more crucial than any detriment to her savings. She remembered seeing a Dunkin' Donuts somewhere in the North End over the course of her four-month hunt around the city for a job and a place to call her own.

Slinging her purse back over her shoulder, she interrupted the closing train doors and surged up the station stairs. Spilling out onto Causeway Street like Jonah emerging from the leviathan's mouth, Diana was pleasantly surprised by her sudden sense of orientation with the city. Knowing precisely where she was and the location of the nearby Dunkin' Donuts. The topography of the city her brain had been mapping for the last four months easily charting the most efficient route to her destination. She ordered a chocolate sprinkle with a large black coffee (extra hot), ignoring the instinctive cringe in her jaw as she paid for it.

Collecting her order, she turned to see a man neatly refold his copy of *The Globe* and set it down on the table. She moved quickly to claim his spot and free newspaper, then sat down intending to open the paper to the classifieds and found herself doing anything to avoid them. She read the funnies. Took her time perusing Arts & Leisure. Even scanned over a column in the sports section questioning Red Auerbach's decision to spend the Celtics' sixth overall pick in the 1978 NBA draft on a young man out of Indiana State by the name of Larry Bird. When Diana realized she'd gone so far out of her way to avoid the classifieds she was feigning interest in sports, she finally admitted defeat on her Boston dreams. Refolding the paper and wiping the sprinkles off the table into her hand, Diana set off down the street in search of a pay phone. A few blocks down, she came across a vacant booth and forced herself inside to make a call she'd been avoiding for weeks.

Shortly after he returned to Stevens Point, Diana's little brother started dating Alicia Zielinski. Despite the new reality of life after his injury, during that time, Diana hadn't seen Aaron happier. It had taken her a while to warm up to Alicia. On the surface, it appeared maybe the most beautiful girl in Central Wisconsin was dating a boy two years younger than her who wouldn't be able to walk for the rest of his life. Granted, Aaron was handsome, and his personality had always possessed a certain magnetism, but something about his injury and Alicia's flawlessness didn't add up. Then one night during the summer of 1974, as dusk illuminated a hazy June sky with a cantaloupe glow, the phone rang at the Hamilton household, and Diana answered. It was Alicia. Diana started to yell for Aaron.

"Actually, I was calling to talk to you."

"Oh. Okay…about what?"

"I thought maybe the two of us could grab lunch sometime. I know your parents moved to Stevens Point after you graduated, and you don't know many people. I get restless here, and I have friends. I'd imagine having only your family to hang out with leaves you pretty stir-crazy. I figured since I'm dating your brother, maybe we could get to know each other a little."

"That's very thoughtful of you."

"Tomorrow at noon at the Cozy Kitchen? Diner food okay?"

Diana found Alicia sitting in a sun-soaked booth, her golden-brown hair pulled back in a bun, her face without makeup. In a way, she was even more beautiful. One of those faces that still held its magic without a mask. It seasoned her attractiveness that she could appear in public without it. Salting it with more solidarity and a peppering of integrity.

Diana took a seat and ordered coffee, sourdough toast and a cup of mixed fruit. Alicia boldly, politely but remorselessly, requested banana pancakes, hash browns, bacon and eggs, which, upon arrival, she laid into with a ravenousness that caught Diana by surprise.

"Do you always eat like this?"

"Like what?"

"Like pancakes and bacon."

"Oh. Uh, yeah…I guess."

"How do you stay so skinny?"

"I don't know, I just do." Alicia shrugged, which annoyed Diana, who felt her hips getting wider every time she ate a sprinkled donut. "Listen, I don't want to be rude, but what is someone like you doing with my brother?

"What do you mean, someone like me?"

"Gorgeous. Older. You've got your whole life ahead of you, and you're dating the only boy in town who can't take you dancing."

"I guess I just like the way he treats me. Most guys either make me feel like a shiny new toy to show off to their friends or they're worshipping at my feet. He just treats me like I'm someone he really cares about. He's smarter than other guys I've dated. He challenges me. And to be honest, I've never really been much of a dancer."

"Is it serious?"

Alicia sat back, glancing out the window again while she chewed on the question and her bacon Diana wished she was eating. "You could say that. I mean, we haven't talked about getting married or anything. We've only been dating a few months. But if you're asking if I take your brother's feelings seriously or not, the answer is I absolutely do."

"So you've considered what it would mean for you to

end up with him? I'm sorry if I'm coming across as pushy, he's just been through a lot this year, and I don't play games when it comes to reality. As someone who's known him his whole life, I can tell you that if he isn't already, he's well on his way to falling in love with you."

"I get it. I'm aware that dating Aaron has some unique obligations, and if it ends up working out, I realize what I'm signing up for. Honestly, I think if anything is going to end our relationship, it's going to be timing."

"Timing? How?"

"I haven't told Aaron this yet. Honestly, I've been putting it off, but I swear I'm going to soon. I got a partial scholarship to attend the University of Washington. My parents offered to help me with the rest. It's a good school, and I've always wanted to go to college on the West Coast. I just didn't think I'd ever be able to find a way to make it possible. So, I'm either going there or UW-Madison. If you'd told me last year I'd even consider dating a guy who'd still be in high school while I went to college, I'd've said you were crazy. If I stay in Wisconsin, I want to give it a shot, and he's a big reason I want to stay in Wisconsin. Seattle, though, I just can't see that working out."

#

Diana discovered a new friend in Alicia that summer. She was intelligent and well-read, which, combined with her beauty, could've made her intimidating, yet somehow, she still emanated an effortless accessibility. Maybe it was her slightly drooping shoulders or her affinity to dress comfortably, but there was an undeniable easiness about her. She wouldn't exactly describe Alicia as warm, she was too sarcastic and straightforward, which Diana came to realize was why she and Aaron worked so well together. They both seemed to have a simple enjoyment of life. Much of their time together that summer was spent around campfires or burning the afternoon on shifty backroad drives with a cassette orbiting in the tape player. They were also both fiercely independent, which was probably why Alicia ended up going to Seattle and why Aaron didn't try very hard to stop her. Though he never talked about it, Aaron was clearly dejected by Alicia's departure. Since the break-up five years ago, there had been a noticeable stagnancy in her brother. Aaron's situation was different than most twenty-three-year-olds with no job who still lived with their parents, when the simple act of getting out of bed and dressed was an hour-long process, but if he ever wanted to get out of Stevens Point and make it farther than a nursing home, he was going to need some prodding. And so, plunging her hand to the depths of her purse, Diana came up with a quarter, fed it in the coin slot, and dialed home. Her mother answered, as usual, wanting to chat.

"It seems like every time I look out the window, it's snowing. I miss looking out and seeing my hummingbirds. Summer always seems to fly by so fast, and winter just pokes along..."

"That's great Mom. I—"

"Layla stopped by earlier today though, that was nice. Arnie got engaged to that girl he met from Spain. Speaking of—have you and Chuck figured out a date for your wedding yet?"

"No we're—"

"Oh honey, I'm so excited you're marrying him! I don't think Aaron expected to like him very much. You know how he feels about 'religious' people, but he said he—"

"Mom! I'm calling from a pay phone and don't want to have to put another quarter in. I need to talk to Aaron. Is he around?"

"I'm sorry honey, I didn't realize—yes, he's here. Aaron!"

"Hello?"

"Hi. How's it going there?"

"Oh…it's going. The cold makes my neck hurt. The snow makes it hard to get out of the house. I'm all tired and restless at the same time."

"Listen, I wanna talk with you about something, and I'm going to be pretty frank."

"You mean like Dr. Frank Magnuson?"

"Cute."

"What's up?"

"I can't afford a place in Boston, and I don't want to move back to Stevens Point again. If I get a place in Milwaukee, I'll at least be near Chuck this summer. Two bedrooms are a lot cheaper than studios if you have a roommate, and you need to get out of Stevens Point. *But…*"

"But?"

"If we live together, I'm not going to be able to help you like Mom and Dad have. I can be there some, but I can't wait on you hand and foot. You're my brother, and I love you, but we have to have some boundaries."

He didn't say anything for a few moments. Then he said, "Alright. But are you gonna throw your Bible at my head every time I drink a beer in the living room?"

"If you can get the bottle open yourself, I suppose you can have as much as you like."

"What about smoking? Can I smoke?"

"I don't know Aaron, it depends on the terms of the lease, but if the landlord allows it, I guess you can smoke in your bedroom."

"Are you going to be this bossy if we live together?"

"I'm not really in the mood for your shit right now. Do you want to live together or not?"

"What did you just say?"

"I said, I'm not in the mood to put up with your crap right now."

"No, you didn't. You said *I'm not in the mood to put up with your shit.* I'm not sure if I want to be associated with a roommate that uses such heathen language." Diana didn't say anything but knew Aaron could hear her feathers ruffling through the phone. "Alright. I'll live with you under the condition that we both agree to respect each other's lifestyles."

"Fine, but that also means you not making so many cracks at the expense of my faith."

"Have you heard the one about the day Jesus and Peter went golfing together?"

"Aaron."

"I'll try."

"I'll be home in a week or so. That'll give you time to start figuring out how you're gonna tackle some of these things without Mom and Dad."

"I've already composed an advertisement for the Journal-Sentinel Personals. Here, tell me what you think…*Aaron— 22, single, white, good sense of humor, in search of mutual business arrangement for sponge baths.*"

"Good one. Bye Aaron."

Diana hung up and walked back to North Station, stopping at a newsstand to treat herself to a pack of wintergreen gum along the way. She took the green line to Back Bay, for the first time enjoying the ride without trying to still the anxious fluttering in her chest. Opening the door of her aunt and uncle's house, she was greeted by the smell of melted butter and lobster. Aunt Gladys standing at the kitchen counter making a salad while Uncle Herman nursed his after-work Manhattan and listened to Duke Ellington in the living room. This was the Boston she loved, the one she'd remember. Familial. Hospitable. Free. Oysters on the half-shell and a smile full of optimism.

CHAPTER 8

When the Church is Being the Church

September 17, 1990—Cheyenne, WY. From the first sermon of Chuck Westerman to Calgary Baptist Church after being diagnosed with a brain tumor.

Chuck: Well, I don't know about you all, but I've had a pretty interesting summer.

Now with apologies to those who have heard this explanation eighty-seven times, I'm gonna give a brief overview of what my summer entailed. First off, this is going to be an interesting day for you because I guarantee this is going to be the most egotistical sermon you've ever heard.

Congregation: *Laughter.*

Chuck: It's also going to be a human sermon. What happened was, late one night in June, I'd driven home from my regular article-writing trip to Ft. Collins. About to fall asleep, I smelled an overwhelming fume from the oil refinery that Bruce works at. The smell was all over the house. It was even outside. Since Diana's nose works much better than mine, even though I've got her beat in size, I decided I'd wake her up to worry her about this.

Congregation: *Laughter.*

Chuck: She went all over the house and outside, got back in bed and declared she could smell...nothing. Well, my first reaction was to worry about her. Then I began to worry about me. What games was my brain playing? Shortly after that, I had a full-fledged seizure, which I have no recollection of because A: I was unconscious, and B: it was too late to borrow a video tape.

Congregation: *Mild, nervous laughter.*

Chuck: I was taken to Cheyenne Regional Medical Center and tested for a few days and told that I had a brain tumor called an astrocytoma. On a malignancy scale of one to four, it was a two. Diagnosis was confirmed at Denver's Swedish Hospital—which, by coincidence, as a complex contains Craig Hospital, where Diana's quadriplegic brother Aaron was rehabilitated seventeen years ago.

The first week of July, I had surgery at Swedish. The few days after the surgery, I was in the ICU and somewhat disoriented, which led, tragically, to my guessing the wrong finalists in the Wimbledon tournament.

Congregation: *Definitive laughter.*

Chuck: Usually I have that nailed. Fortunately, because I'm a pastor, there was no gambling involved.

Congregation: *More laughter.*

Chuck: The surgeon estimated that eighty percent of the cancer had been removed. I was then scheduled for radiation therapy at the nearby Porter Hospital. Over seven weeks, I was to have six thousand units of radiation collected five days a week. This I did, staying weekly in one of the rooms in the Porter Nursing Home reserved for those in treatment at the hospital. I was accompanied most of this time by cross-country friends and relatives who were willing to sacrifice their own schedules and pay huge sums of money for airfare. In return, they took advantage of the opportunity to gong me at Trivial Pursuit for the first time *in their liiives.*

Congregation: *Laughter.*

Chuck: This they felt made the money well spent. Radiation treatment was finished two weeks ago. Some radiologists say that within several weeks, the tiring and other effects of the therapy start to diminish significantly. Others have cautioned that it may be up to a year before complete recovery is felt, even if relatively complete is felt much earlier. Long-term prognosis may be known in a month but may not be fully known for up to six months. The radiologist cautioned that the tumor itself would likely not disappear altogether but would be well into remission. Some statistics I've heard are real optimistic, with a five-year survival rate of ninety percent and a ten-year rate of sixty percent. It may be till the beginning of next year when I'll be given a good sense of my prognosis.

Apart from that, though, I hope to be recovering relatively well, relatively quickly. I hope to be using the American Baptist regional meeting taking place in Cheyenne in a couple of weeks as a beginning return to energy since Earl Clark and I are host pastors, even though I tricked him and made him do all the work.

Congregation: *Laughter.*

Chuck: I'd liked to spend October recollecting my other tasks and be more or less back up to snuff by the beginning of November. If I'm not up to snuff by then, you'll be informed. If I'm up to snuff way before then, I'll whine like a bloodhound, but okay, I'll keep busy.

Congregation: *Crickets...*

Chuck: Now you may be wondering, what can you expect from your pastor? I will tell you right now that things are going to be a little different, at least over the short term. You have spent the last four years trying to stay awake through my sermons. Now it's my turn.

Congregation: *Moderate laughter.*

Chuck: Also, at least for a few months, the haircut stays.

Congregation: *Laughter.*

Chuck: Actually, during the therapy, once the hair started falling out from the radiation, I happened to go to the new movie version of Shakespeare's *Henry V*, and as it turns out, Kenneth Branagh and I have identical hairstyles.

Congregation: *Laughter.*

Chuck: So who's to say that after five hundred years, the style may not come back?

Congregation: *No laughter.*

Chuck: As far as the prognosis goes, the neuropsychologist who spent a couple hours testing me after the surgery was optimistic. He felt like my information recovery would come back well into the ninety percent range. My reaction to, and recovery from, various phases of the medical treatment has been quick. By the same token, I feel as though I should tell you that right now, it takes me longer to get things done than it did before. My memory isn't quite what it was. For reasons that a neurologist perhaps would be able to explain, it seems that sometimes the more recently a piece of information has come into my head, the more likely I am to have a hard time retrieving it. So if you ever think I'm being rude or uncaring because I can't pull something up about you, especially something that came to me not too long ago, please remember that on one occasion, my son Charlie's middle name escaped me altogether.

And him I really care about…

I may get something out and forget where I put it three minutes later. I may schedule a meeting when I had planned on being somewhere else. I'll never be back to normal in a complete sense. On the other hand, consider these things.
A: I'm not sure I've ever been back to normal in a complete sense.

Congregation: *Substantial laughter.*

Chuck: B: Whatever *my* normal is, I've been told I'll be close to back to it—in spite of the hopes of many. C: Going through the church's goofy summer junk mail as swiftly as I did showed me that there are many normal tasks that all your brain never gets used for. D: I'm in the process of—for now—dropping out of some activities that I was doing in addition to my pastoral work before. By the end of the month, I will no longer be the vice president of the Cheyenne Minister's Council. I will no longer be secretary-treasurer of the ministers' council for our Rocky Mountain American Baptist Church region. And I will no longer be a faculty member in the school of religion over at the University of Wyoming. Also, the master's degree in Creative Writing I was working on at UW is on hold for now. I'll be spending the coming vocational year replugging into, and bearing down on, my pastoral work here.

So that's D.

Oh yeah, and E: I really only lost one game of Trivial Pursuit this summer.

Congregation: *Very definitive laughter and even some knee-slapping can be heard through the cassette player.*

Chuck: Okay. So much for a brief recap. Onto the good stuff.

What has been the most stunning feature of my summer vacation? What stood out most notably? Oddly enough, I don't think it's been a malignant brain tumor. Well, okay, that's a real close second. That's like a game behind with maybe a showdown series later. I don't know about you, but I'm not cool enough to be poised and cheerful about scary stuff. And yet, in spite of my normal, human, sniveling reaction to serious medical occurrences, I've been more blown away by the overwhelming, virtually unanimous, and nearly irrational support I have received from other folks in the last few months. I kept waiting and waiting for the disappearance of that support throughout my treatment, but the disappearance never even made it into the ballpark. For that, I am grateful to capacity and awed to my knees. And if I'm also rudely humbled, it's probably because I feel as though I have been given more ministry in the last three months than I've managed to give in four years of being your pastor.

Now please, don't hear this as the standard pat on the head to my world or an overly sentimental rap. I grew up on *Mad Magazine* and *National Lampoon*. Woody Allen is my favorite director. I felt blissfully at home in my spring-semester Mark Twain class. I'm not terribly sentimental.

I am, sometimes, cynical.

I'd rather examine the holes in things than the things themselves. If you would've told me in June, for example, that I would spend a summer in the medical maw, I would've told you that at the end of it, I'd be able to write a biting critique of hospitals. Now there are some small critiques I could make, but I would have to say that my medical experiences have been significantly more positive than I ever would've expected. Friends from all the way back to infancy have been extraordinary. Many have written, not once, but regularly. Many have called, not once, but regularly. I can name four or five who did not spend money on a round-trip ticket here only because we couldn't find a time when someone else wouldn't be here.

Family has been extraordinary. One of my cousins, who's the chief executive of a large eastern hardware firm, volunteered to take a week off to come and be my chauffeur. My wife and young children—they're extraordinary, and the terrible thing is they won't even be snotty about it.

Congregation: *Moderate laughter.*

Chuck: And the church…has been the church.

The church has been, to me, the church. Does that sound like a faint or cynical note of praise? Think. I'm talking about one small situation this morning. One that wasn't even real high on the priority list for the King of the church. It was there, but not real high. He could be saying, "As good as that church did it to that one ordained doofus, I wonder if they could do it to the poor and the sick and the grieving?"

Because I want to say that when the church is being the church—which it so often has the darndest time being—it is being the only thing that's ever going to be forever. When the church is being the church, it's being the only thing that's ever going to be forever. And here's one vote—drop in the ocean though it may be—that the church can, and has, been the church. I've been granted prayer and help from all over the country. From a mass in Arizona to a silent intercession in New Hampshire.

I'm so in debt to the ecumenical church. Nationally, the American Baptist Church has been wonderful. Regionally, the ABC of the Rockies has been more caring than I even have time to go into right now. Here in town, I could point to ways in which the body of Christ in all of Cheyenne has come to me in love and generosity. That brings me to Calgary Baptist Church, the body of which I am a part of.

I'm gonna start with an apology.

I realized very early in the planning of this sharing time that, unlike with chauffeur-wheeling cousins and plane-happy friends, I wasn't going to be comfortable sharing specific examples of ways in which I've been touched by this body. My first concern was that if I even mentioned how one person or family showed me the love of God, it would be inappropriate to stop until I'd acknowledged everyone. My second concern was that if I got started on that, I'd run the risk of going mushy from the pulpit and breaking my four-year record of not doing that and showing what a macho, emotionally controlled adult I am.

Congregation: *Laughter.*

Chuck: Now if that makes you wonder whether your prayers, cards, calls, visits, meals, gifts, conversations, transportations, hugs, baby-sits, sweet comments, jokes I really needed, drawings, patience, taking over my normal chores, suggestions, appropriate back-offs, pretending I wasn't acting weird when I was…and all the other ways you have given to my family that I'm failing to mention, not because I'm not grateful, but because I want you to be able to get home from church before your roast gets dark and dry in the oven. If my non-specificity makes you wonder whether I was touched by all of those or not, let me simply make two observations.

One: I have never had the ministry of Jesus Christ shared with me as I have by this body in the last three months. I have had wonderful pastors. I have been in churches I have loved. I have never had *(getting weak in the throat)* the ministry of Jesus Christ *(welling up)* shared with me as I have by this body in the last three months *(composing himself)*.

That's one.

Two: More broadly and more importantly—this church has reconfirmed not merely by generosity to its pastor, but by the spirit-led work and leadership of so many, this church has confirmed that it is not—as the faith can fall so easily and so dangerously into becoming—a religious clubhouse with an elected activities leader, but rather that this church is a true body through which God's spirit can work.

I don't know who picked this hymn this morning. I guarantee you I didn't give them my two cents about what I was going to be saying, but this hymn has it nailed. This church is a place where folks have been saying, "I'll do thy will, Lord, with a heart sincere. I'll be what you want me to be." This has been a body. This church has demonstrated that it is a true body through which God's spirit can work.

So what happened to me over my summer vacation?

I was led, taught, and touched by the Heavenly Father through the redemption of His Son, through the manifestation of the Holy Spirit that has been made real here by you.

Thank you for your love. Please accept mine.

Congregation: *Standing ovation.*

CHAPTER 9

The Weight of Flying

January 6, 1991—somewhere over the Atlantic on a plane to Bonn, Germany

Paige would miss flying.

Granted, the Bible wasn't too clear on many of Heaven's exact details, but it seemed to convey flying would be part of the deal. In many ways, she imagined that kind of flying would be all the more glorious, what with having your own wings and not having to get to the airport early and all. Still, as she and her mother soared over the Atlantic on the red eye for Paige's second visit to Germany in the last six months, one important exception stirred her doubts—in Heaven, you would know.

Much of the magic she associated with earthly flight was in the mystery. There was no guarantee the plane wouldn't crash. No certainty of what to expect when she landed in a part of the world she'd never been before. But if Heaven was a place where there would be no pain or death, where you learned definitive answers to all the seemingly indefinite questions of life, where your hard-fought faith on Earth in Heaven's promises was rewarded by its making good on those promises—then wouldn't it lose its mysticism?

Probably not.

Living for eternity couldn't be much of a reward if it was going to be boring, but as Paige was still (for the time being) a citizen of the finite, fallen world, it was hard to reason how flying in Heaven would still come with that enrapturing degree of danger which made it so transfixing on Earth.

Her parents had taken the family on road trips to reunions in Arkansas and New Mexico growing up, but until she was seventeen, that was the extent of her travels. An ardent reader from the day Paige learned, the lives described by the occasional visiting missionaries Albin Baptist Church supported, as well as a chip on her shoulder that most educated, hip city secularists thought of religious, small-town people as ignorant and untraveled, all combined to strike her with a serious case of wanderlust. A farm girl from an isolated town, for as long as Paige could remember, whenever her eyes fell on the world map hanging above her father's desk, they were filled with a restless yearning to explore it. Every birthday from fourteen to seventeen came with a twinge of anxiety over not having stuck a single pin in any of the far-off places she wanted to go. In the spring of her junior year of high school, family friend John MacNamee announced in church he'd be leading a three-month mission trip to Peru with Wycliffe Bible Translators. She pounced on the opportunity.

In the months between getting the green light from her parents up until a week before she was set to embark on her journey, Paige was nothing but giddy and confident about her decision. When the time came to actually start packing, however, loud, doubting voices started clamoring in her head. Shouting in unsettling screeches that once she expanded her mind, she could never go back. That once the bubble of a small, familiar world was burst, it could never be un-burst.

The doubts told her to stick with what was comfortable and safe.

These skepticisms came with the forcefulness of a riptide, but ethereal intuition anchored Paige's conviction that her second thoughts were trying to keep her from taking an important and courageous step in her story, so she did her best to ignore the doubts and soldier on with the packing of her bags. The doubts weren't saying anything that would turn out to be particularly untrue, for she really would never be the same after, but Paige knew, in this case, the fear of change was poltroon.

Other than joining Cindy Luther and her dad on a crop-dusting mission once, for all intents and purposes, Peru was Paige's first time flying. When you take off *from* and land *in* the town you've lived in your whole life, it doesn't really count. This was the real deal on a 747, meaning they had to drive two hours down to Denver for their flight. She remembered her stomach feeling like a tangled ball of yarn as the plane taxied down the runway, her heart rate accelerating with the engines as they gathered thrust, the ghostly color of her knuckles strangulating the armrests, then nearly screaming right before takeoff, "Stop this plane and let me off!"

And then...*whoosh!*...the wheels were levitating off the ground. The feeling of instant weightlessness. All becoming calm and transcendent in her spirit as the security of feeling in control was replaced by the freedom of relinquishing it. Since then, she'd always experienced some semblance of that weightlessness whenever a plane finally got off the ground, but that all changed on the flight back from Bonn with Luke after their first visit to the clinic.

#

That first trip to Germany had been…disappointing.

On the flight there, she was full of high hopes and fiery faith. Upon arrival, the doctors shot those hopes down and doused that faith to the point that on their return to Wyoming, Paige willed herself to compile a list of approved names to be her successor as the wife of Luke and mother of Haley and Emma Bainbridge. A list that included former colleagues from their work with InterVarsity back in their twenties, a couple of her old friends from college, one of the girls she'd been a state officer with in Future Homemakers of America, and a handful of women from their church.

For two hours, she wracked her brain, and this was the list she came up with. Looking it over, she noticed some common threads stitched through the character of all these women. All were wise, devout believers, firm in their discipline and generous with their love. Every name on the list was also already married.

She tried hard to justify writing down the names of the single women their age she could think of. Brenda Wilson was a nice enough, church-going woman. Her two boys seemed like decent kids. She was doing the best she could after Don left her for Christie Hatton up in Wheatland four years ago. But she'd never shown Paige much in the way of thoughtful insight in her walk with Christ. Attending the service was merely a part of her weekly routine. The sermon consumed, digested and disposed of by the time she left for work at the bank on Monday. In principle, Brenda agreed with the Gospel's message. In practice, it interfered with her personal wants and so wasn't practiced when practicing lacked convenience. Paige also didn't get the impression

Brenda made it a point to raise her children with an awareness of the world beyond Wyoming. So no. Brenda didn't make the list. When Luke stirred from his nap, she set the list of names on his tray table with trembling hands.

"What's this?"

"Women I think would be a good fit for you and the girls in case I should be unable to complete my matriarchal duties."

"Hmm…" Luke pursed his lips and raised his brow as he made a careful examination of the list. "Well, these are all nice, *married* women."

"I realize that. However, should they become available, I think they'd suit you and the girls well."

"Alright," he said, doubt cracking through his tone. Paige, in turn, betrayed a look of devastation. Taking her hand, Luke added, "Paige Bainbridge—I'd be perfectly happy just being married to you my whole life."

#

In the weeks leading up to her second pilgrimage to Germany, Paige vowed to be a skeptic. She was tired of being disappointed by hope. Unless her very fingers touched the holes where the nails pierced His hands, she wouldn't let herself believe a miraculous healing was possible. Wouldn't let herself imagine making cancer-free, celebratory love to Luke or picture spending time with the girls in the garden instead of her deathbed. The few hours she spent every day with Haley and Emma when they got home from school were of the bitterest bitter and sweetest sweet. Despite being bedridden, they could still do some of their favorite things—watch *Mr. Rogers*, pet the cats, read *The Chronicles of Narnia*. At times, it was quite the cozy little paradise with them up there on her sickbed.

Then there was the hell of the whole situation.

Haley's sullenly inquisitive look when she caught Paige wince and press the button on her morphine pump. The girls fighting each other for the precious individual attention of their mother. The pain it caused having them cuddling up on each side of her becoming too much to tolerate, leaving only one spot directly next to Mom. They'd taken to racing from the school bus to the VIP spot in her bed. It had started off as a giggling, playful competition until the day Paige heard them galloping into her bedroom and Haley tripped Emma, triumphantly running in and leaping on the bed as the shrill cries of her little sister rang out from the den.

Luke was out doctoring a steer with pneumonia, leaving Paige alone to manage the crisis. Her anger toward Haley was as vexing as she'd ever received from her mother. Paige knew from the second she began to administer the tongue lashing it wasn't Haley she was really mad at, and the fact she was taking it out on her made her even more angry and made it even harder to relinquish the verbal whip. Emma walked in, pointing to a fresh, ripe strawberry on her elbow, then pointing accusingly at Haley. Her cheeks even riper than her elbow, the tears and snot gushing out like water from a broken dam. Paige gave Haley a pathetically weak spanking, then used all her remaining strength to pick up Emma and attempt to soothe her with a soft tone of voice and a firm, gentle stroking of the hair. But somewhere in her effort to go from red-hot mad to soft-blue consoling, she herself started crying. For the first time in her life, she silently and directly told God she resented him at that moment. Haley shouldn't have tripped her sister, but she'd only tripped her because she was eight and her mom was too sick and too in pain to have them on each side of her...

And Emma. Sweet, feather-hearted, earnest little Emma. Who, for the majority of her five-year existence, had been nothing but pleasant, bubbling and enthusiastic. Even after Paige got sick, she'd climb willingly in her car seat for another trip to CRMC with gusto. As if every time the minivan started, great adventure lay just beyond. Emma's seemingly endless wealth of energy was going to take her far. It was only a matter of what direction she chose to point her intrepid compass. Though most of the time giggly and optimistic, when warranted, she could weep with the best of them. Getting tripped by Haley had set her off for the common reasons five-year-olds cry, but when Paige started crying, the tune of her youngest's sobs took on a more momentous tone. It made sense to Emma why she herself was crying, but the sight of her mother doing so suddenly brought questions to the surface that had been brooding underneath for months. Why was she always sick? Why couldn't they both just sit on each side of her like they used to? Why did Mom use a walker while Grandma Judith and Grandma Marion got around just fine without one? Why weren't other kids' moms nearly always in bed? She couldn't come up with comforting answers to these questions, and once they'd been asked, it was too late. As Paige tried to soothe her in her lap, she could feel Emma was aware some dark, awful thing had a hold of her mother.

After that day, Paige didn't have to make much effort to tamp her expectations. Over the last month, she'd discovered that underneath the spirit of optimism and belief she'd adopted and fostered ever since Peru, a natural cynic had always lurked beneath. And nothing like month after month of physical suffering coupled with wave after wave of spiritual agony had enabled her Doubting Thomas to surface with such discouraging ease.

If it had always been Paige's fate to die before forty, why did God have to bring Luke and the girls into the whole stinking mess? There was a point about a year after Luke got saved when she'd thought about breaking up again. Not because anything at the time was wrong with their relationship, but simply from a desire for complete independence to roam about the world wherever she pleased through her twenties. The problem was, she loved him so much and couldn't see there being a better man to have children with, so she put her travel plans on hold, figuring she and Luke could travel with more financial freedom someday when the girls were older.

Now she wasn't not going to be around long enough to do any of that.

Until Paige found the lump, she'd always felt a peace about her decision to prioritize family over travel. Now it seemed clear that decision was only going to result in heartache that could've all but been avoided if she'd just left him then and bought a one-way ticket to India. She looked over at her mother zonked out in the aisle seat, strongly suspecting this whole ordeal had been tempting the Thomas in her as well, but the only semblances of a Biblical character Judith Alder had shown her daughter since the diagnosis was Old Testament Joshua. No matter how impractical or saddening the nature of Paige's beck and calls for help, her mother always responded with that almost obnoxiously positive *be strong and courageous!* attitude. But when Paige pictured her mother in moments alone, she reckoned the sorrow was more than Judith could bear.

Like Luke and the girls, being the source of her parents' heartache made it that much harder for Paige to stave off bitterness. Still, if not for their actions and attitude throughout the last two years, she probably would've gone Thomas a lot sooner. Despite their noble efforts, it looked like they were going to end up losing their daughter to bitter skepticism in the end. The fracture Emma's smile suffered the day Haley tripped her had fractured something in Paige as well. She rescinded her declaration of disdain for her Heavenly Father shortly after making it, but they didn't talk much these days. She'd been in prison too long to still be singing.

Shifting her eyes past her mother, Paige peered out the east-facing window to see the first glints of daybreak stabbing through the ebony veil of night. A month ago, she would've watched and tried to be thankful for the promise of sunrise, but that morning she pushed the button on her morphine pump and tried to get some sleep.

#

Shortly after dozing off, her nap was interrupted by her mother's resolute hand nudging her shoulder. "Paige! Wake up!"

"What's going on?"

"We're almost there. Look out the window."

Paige wearily complied with the request…and she had to admit, the sky before them was about as beautiful as she could remember. One of those divinely golden and coral-beamed sunrises—flaxen fingers of early daylight working through cottony, blushing clouds to grace the earth with their touch. And yet, she fought the pull to admire the dawn's beauty. To do that meant admiring her Creator. But for the first time since Haley tripped Emma, she had to fight an inclination to smile despite her circumstances. Her seat was adjacent to the left wing of the plane, the tip of it pointing directly at the heart of the rising sun, and just as Paige was about to look away, the motion of the cabin seemed to freeze. In the window's faint reflection, she saw herself, not as she was at that moment, but as she did on her flight back from Peru.

She could see herself at seventeen, looking out the window as they dropped back into Denver, the look of a pretty blonde girl from Albin, Wyoming, being rewarded with the satisfying self-realization that little Paige Alder had successfully crossed the equator and back.

As they descended upon Bonn, it occurred to her that trip to Peru had been her first real grownup act. The rite of passage to her womanhood. The equivalent of a farm girl's vision quest. She'd gone to Peru to see if the transformation of the soul Jesus promised would be rewarded to His faithful, and she'd found it among the Aguaruna people in one of the world's most remote jungles. Their mission was not a misguided, arrogant attempt to Westernize the Aguaruna culture. They'd gone humbly to help the tribe understand the Gospel by sharing in the practical struggles of their day-to-day lives and relating to them with respect and love as human beings.

Those three months had their share of homesick moments. Her main assignment had been translating hymns into the language of the Aguaruna. Though not as physically taxing as clearing a quarter-mile airstrip in the meat of the jungle with one semi-functioning chainsaw and a few machetes (the work the boys had been given), mentally, it had been a grueling labor of love. The language barrier, in general, was challenging, as was the excessive heat, multitudinous biting insects and lack of plumbing and electricity. But her experiences in those three months were truly revelatory. It didn't take long to realize she had as much to learn from the Aguaruna as she had to teach them. Though centuries behind technologically, their self-resourcefulness was ages ahead of the modern world. She marveled at watching the women spin and weave their cotton into hammocks, rich in color and elaborately patterned. She cherished the primitive opulence of Chief Tadeeti's infamous crimson and gold feather hat and the generous heart he showed in giving it to John MacNamee as a gift for their work helping clear the airstrip. One night, Paige accepted an invitation from a family in the tribe to eat dinner at their home. They had tapir in her honor, a gamey, jungle-dwelling hog that tasted like it'd been marinated in hot garbage, but she left their meager thatched hut astounded by how much people of such different languages and cultures shared in common.

Among the Aguaruna, she learned the meaning of true faith—one that permeates your whole being and gives you hope and resilience in a world that feels somewhat off its axis.

As the plane lowered through the ceiling of clouds to reveal a brilliant view of Deutschland, Paige was reminded of the crippled man being lowered through the roof by his friends in Mark's Gospel. How when Jesus saw their faith, he first said to the paralyzed man, "Your sins are forgiven." And how the paralyzed man was probably like, "That's great rabbi! Now how about healing my legs?" If she ascribed to the Gospel, there was no getting around the order of this. Jesus was foremost concerned with healing the soul. Surrender daily your pride and self-serving agenda, and your spirit will be restored. True, he did heal the crippled man lowered through the roof that day, but what about those who couldn't walk almost two centuries later? At first logic, it seemed essential he heal both soul and body to prove his love, but a second thought considered the fact that plenty of perfectly healthy people have lived miserably selfish and unfulfilling lives. Paige hadn't, but she couldn't claim to be her own savior. She'd grown up with two parents who loved her and each other, who modeled finding contentment in daily life and helping their neighbor. They weren't perfect parents or perfect people, but she could never question their honest effort to model the love of Christ in her life.

Growing up around their faith influenced her greatly, but it wasn't until she went to Peru that faith became her own and thoroughly had an impact on her life. That Paige—seventeen and brimming over with belief—stared at her now in the reflection of the window and asked if her faith was in Heaven or on this earth?

She realized if her answer was the latter, if her hope was in flying on Earth, then there wasn't much difference between her faith and Brenda Wilson's.

CHAPTER 10

The Mile-Wide City

*January 6, 1991—Denver, CO,
Swedish Medical Center*

It felt like twenty years since the nurse had told them the doctor would be in shortly.

"I can't believe I'm back here," Diana thought aloud to Chuck as they waited for Dr. Halsey. Chuck nodded aloofly, nervously scratching the back of his weary head. He hadn't had any more seizures, but the headaches were back, and it was enough to put them on edge.

They call Denver the Mile-High City. To Diana, it felt a mile wide—between Craig Hospital, where Aaron had gone for rehab after the accident, and the adjacent Swedish Medical Center, where she and Chuck were about to be told whether or not his cancer was still in remission. For the life of her, Diana couldn't fathom how both facilities managed to be located next to each other in one convenient square mile of Hell.

She glanced down at her watch. It was nine in the morning, ten in West Allis, the Milwaukee suburb where Aaron lived. They'd been waiting for Dr. Halsey for almost a half hour. Her brother was probably out of bed and dressed now, drinking his second cup of Folger's Instant and beginning his workday as a landlord for a nine-unit apartment. He'd purchased the same building—still lived in the very same unit—Diana had found after she called him in Boston. The same apartment the three of them all shared for six happy weeks after Chuck graduated from Dartmouth.

In the eighteen years since Aaron's accident, he'd become a legend at Craig Hospital and a banner of hope for future quadriplegics. A fully independent quad was as rare a phenomenon as a total solar eclipse.

He was that total eclipse of the sun.

While they wait for Dr. Halsey, Diana rummaged through the cluttered attic of long-ago memories and pieced together details of her first visit to Craig during Christmas 1973. Grammie Mitchell had been there. Her late husband, Harris Mitchell, was the director of the YMCA in Mt. Vernon, Ohio, where Bea—their middle daughter—discovered and explored her love for swimming and other outdoor recreation. Once every few summers, Harris brought Peggy (his wife, aka Grammie Mitchell) and their three daughters to the YMCA of the Rockies in Estes Park, Colorado, for a week. The day after Christmas 1973, Grammie Mitchell took Diana to Estes Park to show her the Y. Many particulars of that afternoon were fuzzy, but she had a clear image of mountains evaporating in low, overcast clouds. At the time, at least, she thought they were mountains. Later she'd learn they were merely the foothills, but Diana had never seen mountains like the Rockies. The foothills themselves struck her as colossal and awe-inspiring enough for a girl from the plain-level fielded woods of the Midwest. Per Grammie's suggestion, she returned to the YMCA of the Rockies the following June as a member of the summer staff. This time no cumulous shroud concealed the young stone behemoths towering beyond the foothills. Their majesty stirred a yearning in Diana to become more intimate acquaintances. That summer, she spent the majority of her free time hiking betwixt the peaks with others from the camp staff. There was something sacred and healing in that unsullied, coniferous air. The drastic grace of the lofty, muscular earthen pinnacles. The sanctuary stillness and prodigious posture of the young and handsome Rockies. All its geologic complexities coming together to pull on deep, simple things in her soul. Recalling in her a gratefulness for the meeting of primitive needs like the breathing of fresh air or the taking of a cool drink on a shaded rock after a moiling morning hike. She relished the purity of enjoying a spectacular view, a good conversation with a friend, a handful of trail mix, the plunging of perspiring feet in a crisp mountain stream.

She couldn't get enough.

Diana had been accepted to the Moody Bible Institute in Chicago, but she finagled the admissions office to let her start in the spring so she could help Aaron and her parents get acclimated with their new way of incomplete-quadriplegic life. Her love affair with the Rockies was put on hold the following summer as the Moody Glee Club offered her an opportunity to take a six-week, dirt-cheap singing tour of Europe. Though she admired the Alps, her ultimate affections remained bound to the Rockies. She transferred again in the fall of '75 to Trinity Baptist College in Deerfield, Illinois, where she planned to complete her BA in psychology. The following summer, she returned to Estes Park and found her feelings for the Rockies weren't just a passionate fling, but a sustaining love. Then, back in Waukesha at a New Year's Party her senior year, she ran into Katie Westerman, an old friend from church camp, and, "Oh by the way, do you remember my little brother Chuck?"

They started dating a week later and persevered through the long distance that spring. Then Chuck—not wanting to squander his opportunity with a girl who was better looking than him, in many ways just as smart and in some, smarter (as he would later tell her)—pounced on Diana's offer for him to join her in Estes Park that summer. His job in the camp maintenance department didn't exactly suit his talents or ideas of enjoyable work, but he agreed with his girlfriend on the beauty of the mountainous West. They wouldn't return again until the summer of '82, this time working as camp counselors under the title of Mr. and Mrs. Westerman. By then, Chuck had worked his way to the Assistant Director of the C.Y.C.L.E. Youth Program in Chicago and was set to start the following autumn at Northern Baptist Theological Seminary. Diana, who had started at C.Y.C.L.E. with Chuck, left after a year to pursue a graduate degree at the Illinois Institute of Technology. Upon completion, she used her freshly stamped Master's in vocational rehabilitation to land a job at the Rehabilitation Institute of Chicago, working as a counselor for people with spinal cord injuries and other physical and mental impairments.

As Chuck neared the end of seminary, he started applying to pastoral jobs in areas of the country he and Dye thought would be a good fit. Chicago, Milwaukee and Pennsylvania, based on familial ties and established peers, as well as the Mountain West, based on their fond memories at the YMCA of the Rockies. They got offered positions in all three areas east of the Mississippi. Not bad offers, but the gut feeling of conviction wasn't there. When Calgary Baptist Church in Cheyenne finally called, it seemed right for reasons both practical and romantic.

It was almost as if Aaron had led them there—within a hundred miles of one of the best brain tumor centers in the country. As a knock finally landed on the door of their hospital room, Diana Westerman asked God for her brother's injury to be the thing that allowed her husband to live.

#

Dr. Halsey entered, and Chuck didn't care for the overcast look on his face. "I'm sorry to say it's come back."

Silence permeated the room like alcohol poured into a deep cut. Chuck stared down at his shoes, remembering back to their Chicago days when he used to use duct tape to hold them together. The kids from Cabrini Green Public Housing he had been there to help liked to razz him for that. "Yo Chuck! You need new shoes man! Chuck! You need new shoes!"

He always found that funny. It would've made a good sermon illustration somehow, but he knew after what Dr. Halsey just said he wasn't going to be giving any more of those.

"Do I have another pea in my brain?"

"I'm afraid this one's about the size of a golf ball."

"I hate golf. I think too much to be any good at it. If only I had a brain tumor, I wouldn't have to think so much."

"What now?" Diana asked, ignoring him.

"Since the tumor is much larger than the first, operating on it would mean a significant loss of speech, both severe long and short term memory loss, as well as a drastic change in personality and intelligence…to be honest, he'd be more like a carrot than a husband."

"Ha! A pea brain in a carrot body. All you need is a meathead and you've got yourself a human pot roast! Funny Doc! Funny."

"Chuck. He wasn't *being* funny."

"I know. It's not funny. I speak and write and relate to people for a living, so having a surgery that significantly impairs my ability to do those things might be problematic. Would you rather I start tearing my clothes and pulling out my hair?"

"What do we do if you can't remove it?"

"It's a big tumor. We can try radiation but—"

"But what?"

"I'm afraid the odds of it being successful are less than one percent."

"I want another option."

"Chuck, I'm sorry, but you've probably only got about three to six months."

"Until I can play golf?

"No, I mean you've only got three to six months to—"

"I know what you mean."

"Do you want my advice?"

"Go golfing?

"Make the most of the time you have left. Take your wife on a nice vacation. Somewhere with a beach."

CHAPTER 11

Sticking it to Dr. Frank Magnuson

January 6, 1991—West Allis, WI, Aaron's Apartment

Each morning since he'd moved into his West Allis apartment in the fall of 1979, Aaron awoke to see his chair parked within arm's reach of his bedside. A multitude of barriers stood between him and his beloved morning cup of Folgers Instant Coffee. It would be a beautiful struggle to witness if anyone were ever around to witness it. A triumph of mental fortitude and scrupulously calculated physical maneuvers. Since the injury caused the muscles in his legs to spasm at night, they were held down by a leather strap cushioned with sheepskin that attached to a nylon rope and pulley system of his own design. Some quads got abrupt, thrashing spasms. Aaron's occurred more like a surfacing submarine—slowly, methodically. If his legs weren't strapped down, his knees would gradually levitate to his chest. Without the straps, Aaron would end up on his side in the fetal position, unable to jostle himself out of bed.

Casting off the covers and exposing his body to the winter morning chill, he slackened the rope and pulley to free his legs, then disconnected his catheter from the rubber hose connected to the bed bag before commencing the scuffle. Using the heels of his palms to clasp a leather string looped through a thirty-by-eight-inch transfer board, he stationed the board between the bed and his chair to form a small wooden bridge. Double-checking to ensure the brakes on his chair were set, he inched himself to the mattress's edge with his hands, then docked his person parallel to the mother ship.

Now came the cruxy part.

If he rushed the transfer and fell off the board, his whole morning and potentially afternoon would be spent pleading loudly through the walls for one of his tenants to come and assist him off the floor, not to mention the bruises his body would wear for months. The physics of it all had to be executed with patient precision to avoid disaster. An orchestration of bracing, leverage and inching momentum. No motion of his body was made without considerable effort and the application of Aaron's mind. Every move was calculated. The placement of his hands on the parts of the chair with the most structural integrity. The dogged shifting of his weight across the bridge. His limbs all the while shivering from the cold and shaking like a broken motor when strained at certain points from the injury. Still, an innate sense of triumph came every morning when he finally got his slender, bony ass in the seat of that intrepid chair.

Aaron Hamilton—one. Dr. Frank Magnuson—zero.

Frankly, Frank, there was a huge, considerable difference between complete and incomplete quads, limited dexterity, or none at all. The difference that allowed him just enough mobility to function in a manual chair instead of an electric, to get through his day on his own and eventually buy the very nine-unit apartment building Dye signed them a lease for five years before he put his elementary signature down on the title to become a landlord.

During the years he lived at home with his parents after the injury, he and his father worked together industriously—shaping wood, tailoring leather, bending metal to design various instruments for Aaron to live independently. Once they'd invented the basics to get around the everyday utilitarian obstacles of Aaron's handicap, he was free to pursue more thrilling challenges and innovations. Participating in competitive wheelchair races all across the country through the mid-eighties—among his teammates and fellow competitors, Aaron's injury was the most severe. Even they could hardly believe his ability to travel such long distances alone—his only assistance being the array of gear he'd custom designed. Over the next decade, he schemed up inventions and methods that allowed him to hunt, fish, camp and kayak. One of his proudest achievements being the customized twenty-two-caliber rifle with a specialized tripod and a trigger he could hold between his teeth and pull by biting down.

During this time, he also began conducting seminars for other paras and quads, sharing his techniques for living an active and independent chair-bound life. From an immaterial standpoint, in the eighteen years since his accident, Aaron had lived a wildly successful life. Materially, a leg up had proved hard to achieve.

In the winter months, he wore loose-fitting long-sleeve shirts. He hadn't worn underwear in years—another grappling task to perform that interfered with his leg bag. He always liked to see the look on people's faces when he told them he hadn't bought new underwear since the Ford administration. If it made them uncomfortable, that was their problem. It was funny, and if Aaron was going to continue to beat Dr. Magnuson's odds, a healthy morbid sense of humor was vital.

Wrestling his unmoving legs through a pair of relaxed-fit Levi's, he wriggled them up to his waist. His remaining dexterity wasn't enough to button them, so he'd invented what looked like a miniature shepherd's crook—a six-inch dowel handle with a small brass hook attached to the end. He put the hook through the buttonhole, slipped it through the top half of the button, then carefully pressed it through the bottom. Once accomplished, he laced the hook through the hole in the fly and...

Zzzip!

It took about twenty minutes from the moment Aaron threw off the covers to the time he got his black hooded sweatshirt on. The warmth that came with accomplishing this task was one of a handful of daily moments he found a simple grace in life that never occurred to most able-bodied people. Though it was a grace short-lived because then came the real challenge. Bending down to the floor, he hooked a finger through the heel loop attached to a left Asics wrestling shoe, set it next to his feet, then did the same with the right. Shoes without heel loops were nonnegotiable in Aaron's world. If he bought a pair that didn't have them, he'd stitched on a set of his own with his mother's old sewing machine—modified, of course, for his purposes. The silver-dollar-sized holes he cut in the soles of the wrestling shoes served to relieve pressure sores. Since being a quad required an ungodly amount of sitting, he was easily prone to them. Poor circulation was another condition of his injury, making wounds like pressure sores a real bitch, as his crawling blood slowed the healing process to a drawling pace and left him vulnerable to infections.

Cutting the holes took the pressure off his heels.

Low-top shoes had a tendency to slide off in the tussle during his pickup transfers. The extra high tops of the wrestling shoes ensured they stayed on and protected his ankles when he made the transfers. Once, during the six weeks when Chuck and Dye lived with him, he was transferring out of his pickup in a pair of low tops and, in the slightest moment of negligence, shellacked his ankle against the metal leg of his chair. It bruised like a giant peach and three months later looked like one would if it sat in a fruit bowl that long without being eaten. This was back in his youth, when he was more prone to committing the two cardinal sins of an independent quad—impatience and carelessness. Committing either of these sins violated the golden rule of Aaron's life—don't compound the problem.

In addition to their anti-bruising function, the high-tops gave better support and leverage to push his heel down while he held the shoe by the loop until the ball of his foot finally reached the cut-out sole. The wrestling shoes were also easier to cut holes in the bottom of and provided the flexibility needed to get them on without being too flimsy. A functional, long-lasting set of shoes were a better friend to Aaron than Jesus. The stiffness of a new pair could turn the task of getting them on into a twenty-minute affair. People wouldn't think a guy who hadn't walked in eighteen years would have to fret much about shoes.

People didn't have a clue.

Alas, his current pair were well-worn, still sturdy, and today he got them on in under five. Aaron Hamilton—2. Dr. Frank Magnuson—0.

The income from his apartments provided with him enough to barely get by. It would've been nice to heat every room in his unit during the day, but if he wanted to save enough to finally buy a house, heating his bedroom that doubled as an office was all he could afford. His ambition was to someday sell the whole building, buy a house, and still have enough left in his savings to live the rest of his days in modest comfort. Just something with no stairs, two bedrooms, a garage and a backyard. He could put his office in the spare room along with a guest bed so his parents and nephews didn't have to sleep on the living room futon when they visited. The garage would provide a workspace other than his current second bedroom, which he'd converted into a workshop for carpentry projects and restoring old Studebaker motorcycles. The yard just needed to be big enough to fit a charcoal grill and a fire pit so he could have friends over for beers and brats in the summer.

Shoving his cigarettes into the pouch of his sweatshirt, Aaron wheeled down the hall to the kitchen. Off the custom-built thigh-high countertop, he hooked his fingers through a golden mug stamped with a large brown horse and rider Diana had sent him after she and Chuck moved to Wyoming. It came with a packet of chili seasoning and a note written in calligraphic handwriting:

Made sure it was a good thick one so you don't burn your hands! Chuck found this chili seasoning in some little town close to Cheyenne he went through on his way to a ranch to herd cattle on horseback. Chuck on a horse—picture that! Anyway, it's pretty tasty. Thinking of you... Lots of love, Dye.

Aaron looked skeptically at the packet of seasoning after he got the package. *World-Famous Chugwater Chili—Chugwater, Wyoming,* he read. "World-famous, my crippled ass. If it's really world famous, you don't have to announce it to the world because they already know about it."

He filled the mug with water, ready to nuke it in the microwave, when the phone rang. It was Dye. Crying like a widow. Chuck had another tumor. This one the size of a golf ball. Inoperable. Three to six months. Fuck. He never thought his sister would marry someone he could tolerate, let alone genuinely like. When she first told him she started dating a guy who she'd met back in high school at church camp, Aaron rolled his eyes. When she said he was planning to attend seminary, he was even more pessimistic.

But he liked Chuck.

Hell, he loved the goofy, brilliant bastard. One of a handful in the world who could actually match wits with Aaron and the only ordained minister he knew who didn't look at him like he was going to Hell. When they lived together those six weeks, on Saturday nights they'd watch *SNL* and drink a couple Millers. One night after Aaron had more than a couple, he fell out of his chair laughing. "Chuck! Help me up! I'm so drunk I can't even walk."

He'd never forgotten the sound of the laugh coming from Chuck. An understanding chuckle if ever he'd heard one. That was the moment he realized he loved his God-fearing brother- in-law.

"So this is how you repay a guy who could've been a Wall Street lawyer but decided to spend his prime in duct-taped shoes teaching poor kids how to read?" Aaron said to a God he didn't believe in after hanging up with Dye. "Take up your mat and walk, my crippled ass."

He finished nuking the water for his coffee, stirred in a spoonful of Folgers, and wheeled outside to smoke. Flicking the lighter with the heel of his palm, he took a long, steady drag, the cindering tobacco hitting his brain with a jolt of electric nicotine, jumpstarting further memories of that summer living with Diana and Chuck…

That perfect August evening when they went to see REO Speedwagon at Summerfest downtown. Despite getting there only five minutes before the opening song (thanks to Diana), they were able to finagle their way to the front (thanks to Aaron). About halfway through the show, his nose caught a forgotten but familiar scent, followed by a familiar voice calling, "Aaron?" close behind him.

It had been years since he'd heard his name in that way—like it was coated in the sweetest honey. He wheeled around, not ready to believe what he knew he'd find—tanned, willowy legs, a lissome nose constellated faintly with freckles, dangling shoulders, which somehow always made her neck more alluring, and yes, a hint of strawberry shampoo lingering in the summer night air. They stood there for a long moment, not saying anything as Kevin Cronin started in on the first verse from "Only the Strong Survive."

> *You may not know this, but you are everything you've ever needed*
> *Heaven with a touch of New York, silver with a touch of gold*
> *And I can see where you're goin', but I don't really know the way*
> *It's got too many changes, too much rearranging,*
> *Too many ways to go astray*
> *So if you wanna go, let me go along*
> *I never walked that road alone*
> *I heard it was hard*
> *I heard it was long*

But we'll come back alive
Cause only the strong survive

After Alicia went to college, she stopped by the Hamiltons' to see him a few times a year when she came home. Just friendly visits. The University of Washington had a good nursing program, and through that, she'd met Gary Stedman in the fall of her sophomore year. Gary Stedman. Aaron had met him once when he came home with her for Christmas. He didn't know Gary was going to be at the Zielinskis' when he went over to listen to records with Ty. Gary Stedman. Nice guy. Pre-Med. Slightly above average looking. Huge dork. Was going to be a pediatrician, and man, it was probably a good thing Aaron was physically unable to have to resist the impulse to crush every bone in Gary Stedman's pale, floppy, West-Coast hand when he shook it. She dated that goober for three years until the summer of '78. Through Ty, Aaron learned she'd broken up with him when it turned out that Mr. Nice Guy was actually a neurotic control freak in the end. Shortly after that, she landed a job at Aurora St. Luke's Medical Hospital in Milwaukee.

"You should look her up when you get there dude. I know she'd love to see you," Ty told Aaron when he came over to help him move.

"Yeah, maybe…" Aaron replied. His chest had jumped when he heard she'd broken up with Gary, followed by a sinking reminder that she'd chosen maybe the worst profession Aaron could think of if they were ever going to have another shot. The last thing she'd want to do after a twelve-hour shift was come home to someone else who needed help. Nevertheless, there she was, the Milwaukee skyline draped in rosy dusk behind her. Looking at him with that look. Her blue-green eyes careening through him.

And he'd known then how it would turn out. That the rest of summer would be the happiest time of his life. There wasn't a weak relational link between the four of them. Alicia and Dye picked up their friendship where they left off. With her love for reading books by old or dead British guys, she and Chuck took to each other right away. Even after Chuck and Dye moved to Chicago to start at C.Y.C.L.E., in the following weeks, Aaron pensively enjoyed the bittersweetness of their autumn-splendor love. Like the leaves bursting with color before their death, he knew that the spark-flying night he and Alicia happened upon each other at Summerfest would be enough to rekindle their love, but would eventually surrender to the resentment he felt dating the gorgeous saint who cared for sick people and her charity-case boyfriend. He knew he should've never started back up with her, but her radiance that night trumped his better judgment.

#

Stubbing out his cigarette and wheeling back inside to start the day's work, Aaron could still feel her cloying pleas sticking to his living room walls from the night she'd spoken them over a decade ago.

"I don't care. I don't care. I don't care! I don't care that you can't walk. I love you. You could be blind and paralyzed and I'd still love you. Don't you get it? This is what I want. I don't feel obligated to be with you, it's something I've chosen to do, and I'm happy. *You* are who I want."

"This is what you want right now. Trust me Leash, in ten years, you'll wish you hadn't. This is what's best for you."

"I should be the one to decide what's best for me. And

what about you? What about what's best for you?"

"I'll be fine. I love you, but you deserve better."

Yes, Aaron Hamilton had pushed Alicia Zielinski away right back into the arms of a "changed" Gary Steadman, who changed long enough for them to marry and have a son before he started taking his frustration with children dying under his care out on Alicia by getting drunk and knocking her around the room. By 1988, she and her son, Lionel, had left him. Last Aaron knew, they were living in Denver. Aaron himself had dated a handful of women since Alicia. Broken women whose love he felt worthy of, but whose faces could never escape the shadow of Alicia Zielinski. He went back to Craig for a checkup in the summer of '89 and debated calling her to get together, but the thought of trying to love Gary Steadman's kid made him put the phone down...

You're a damn fool Aaron Hamilton, he thought to himself as he wheeled to his desk, then started looking over the onerous bills for the apartment building.

CHAPTER 12

The Truth Is Marching On

February 18, 1991—First Baptist Church, Chugwater, WY

It wasn't easy, but Paige had made it.

There she was, back to one of her great, pure joys—seated at the church piano, the offering plates about to be passed from hand to hand by her community, their dutiful hearts giving their ten percent along with a humble prayer for good rain and no hail to batter their hard-toiled harvest. She'd decided on "Battle Hymn of the Republic," knowing her father-in-law would be there and that it was his favorite. Aside from her tenderness for Kirk Bainbridge, the triumphant tone of the piece appealed to her in the midst of her discouraging situation.

"Before I start," she said, addressing the congregation. "I'd just like to say how glad and honored I am to still be able to do this. It's no secret this has been a difficult last couple years for our family, but we're so blessed to have your overwhelming love, support and ceaseless prayers. I want to thank you for that, wholly and truly. I don't know where we'd be without you."

Dear friends' eyes welled. Weathered old ranchers'

graying heads nodded with understanding. Elderly agrarian wives lips formed in encouraging, pain-acknowledging smiles. They all knew it was very well the last time they'd get to hear Paige play. Fixing her eyes on the sheet music before her composure could be compromised, she drew a deep breath, then she counted herself in and thrust down on the keys. The first exultant chord burst out in a jubilant reunion, throwing its sonic arms around Paige like a friend she hadn't seen for a long time but picked up with right where they last left off.

With ease and release, she played the first verse and chorus while the faux-gold grooved plates snaked their way across the aisles. As she went into the chorus the second time around, a moment was created so unscripted and wonderful she couldn't contain a hearty chuckle as Walt Clark, the ever-sage, retired, former pastor of Chugwater First Baptist Church had risen to his feet, bellowing out the battle cry in his rumbling, soulful baritone—G<small>LORY</small>, <small>GLORY</small>, <small>HA-LLE-LUUU-JAHHH</small>! G<small>LORY</small>, <small>GLORY</small>, <small>HA-LLE-LUUU-JAHHH</small>! G<small>LORY</small>, <small>GLORY</small>, <small>HA-LLE-LUUU-JAHHH</small>! H<small>IS TRUTH IS MARCHING OOON</small>!!!

Others rose to their feet and joined in. Grace and Carol, Kirk and Marion, Paige's parents, Marcy Black, Luke, Haley and Emma, until eventually the whole congregation was on their feet singing with all their might, joyful and undefeated. And for five minutes, no trace of the doubt and frustration they'd gone through together could be found in that meager, wood-paneled sanctuary. For five minutes, Paige Bainbridge wasn't sick and powerless. In that moment, she and her brothers and sisters in Christ became, as the Apostle Paul wrote, more than conquerors—almighty and brimming over with a belief in the ultimate victory of love.

When she struck the final chord, a roar of applause and cheers erupted from the forty-or-so souls in the room as Grace helped her down the steps to her walker. The momentum of the victory carried over through Pastor Ted's sermon as the words spilled off his tongue with truth and passion. It trickled below to the basement as they cascaded down the steps to gather for the potluck. Judith came to the house the night before and helped Paige make chicken tortilla casserole, which was already gone by the time Doug Duncan got to it, much to his indignation.

"Tim!" he exclaimed to the bowlegged man ahead of him in line. "You've got two scoopfuls of that casserole on your plate there the size of Texas. At least let me have a bite or two."

"Partner—the only way you're getting a lick of this casserole is if you install one of your HydraBeds on my pickup for half cost."

"Done!" Doug exclaimed, thrusting his fork into the creamy heap of goodness.

And for one triumphantly graceful afternoon, for the first time since Paige felt the lump, she felt like more than a conqueror, more than the earthbound body she'd been reduced to.

CHAPTER 13

The Beautiful Lady in the Red Sundress

February 18, 1991–Kona Island, HI

Chuck knew it was his last birthday.

He didn't know that ten years from the day, Dale Earnhardt Sr. would get forced into the wall on turn four at Daytona International Speedway and never live to tell about it or see Junior win a race. But Chuck knew thirty-four would be his last birthday. Over the last month, he'd grown weak enough to need a wheelchair most of the time, which had him thinking about Aaron a lot, and thinking about Aaron meant thinking about Dale Earnhardt Sr., because Aaron never loved a driver of his favorite sport more.

Chuck's bet had always been on dying at eighty-four, but he was trying to be thankful he'd only overestimated that number by fifty and not more. God had given him one more year than His own son, so he was trying to take some measure of comfort in that. All he wished for his last birthday was to find the beautiful lady in the red sundress, and that didn't seem like much to ask.

He'd looked everywhere but couldn't find her.

"Excuse me?" Chuck asked, approaching the girl working the gift shop register in his wheelchair, somewhat aware he didn't look like your typical Hawaiian tourist. The wispy mustache and roughly shaven head. The steroid-bloated face and chubby neck ill-suited with the rest of his gangly frame. His garb even more ill-suited—tattered, white Chuck Taylor's, a pair of golden yellow University of Wyoming sweatpants with bucking horse-n-riders down the left side and a blue threadbare shirt with a cancer foundation logo on the front and Miller Lite emblem on the back.

"Yes?" She smiled sweetly, but with some reluctance. Her feathery caramel-and-honey-colored hair and long, pretty cheeks seemed fitting for the "Heather" on her name tag.

"I'm looking for the beautiful lady with the long dark hair and the b-b-big red sundress. I came in here yesterday and she was over there..." he managed to spit out at a snail-like pace, pointing to the far wall of the store. "But now I can't find her."

"Do you happen to know her name?"

"Name? No...she's an-an..." Over the last six months, his once impressive mental thesaurus had been reduced by sixty percent, so instead of fishing the word *ornament* out of his vernacular, instead he said, "She's an object."

"Hmmm. Was she a customer, or did she work here?"

"What? No. She was for purchase."

"Are you sure you're in the right store, sir?"

"This is the only gift shop in the hotel, isn't it?"

"Yes."

"Then I'm sure this is where I saw her—yeah. Right next to those t-t-tacky shirts with the flowers on them."

"Was anybody else with you?"

"My wife."

"Your wife?"

"Yes, my wife. She loved her. That's why I want to buy her."

"I see…so where's your wife now?"

"At the beach. She thinks I'm taking a nap. I'm going to surprise her."

"Hmmmm…"

"Believe me, she could use a nice surprise."

"What about getting her a purse?"

"Do you have any that could carry a twenty-five-pound watermelon?"

"I don't think we do…"

"Those are the only kind of purses she likes. The woman doesn't ex-exactly p-p-pack light."

"Maybe some nice earrings?"

"I'm no good at b-buying her jewelry," he stammered. "How you ladies decide between which earrings are *nice* and which aren't is beyond me. As long as you're sm-smiling, they could be made of shark teeth and look nice to me. Can you just ch-try and help me find the lady in the sundress? I know my wife will like her because she told me she did."

"What room are you in sir?"

Chuck huffed. What room is he in? "315…I think."

"Okay, and what's your wife's name?"

"Diana. Please don't call her. I want it to be a surprise."

Heather picked up the phone sheepishly and called room 315, where a frumpy-sounding woman named Grace answered and said that no damn Diana was staying there.

"What's your last name sir?"

"Westerman."

She picked up the phone again and dialed the front desk. "Hey Dom, it's Heather. Can you tell me what room a Diana

Westerman is staying in? 513? Great. Thanks."

When Heather looked up from the phone, Chuck was no longer in front of her but wheeling away acrimoniously toward the far wall and mumbling obscenities. The phone in room 513 was barely through its first ring when Diana answered anxiously.

"Hello?!?"

"Hi. Is this Mrs. Westerman?"

"Yes."

"Um, I've got your husband here in the gift shop."

"Thank heavens! Is he alright?"

"Yes, he's fine…he, well, he seems to be a little out of sorts. He keeps talking about finding some beautiful woman in a red sundress. I, uh, hope I'm not getting in the middle of anything."

"Just an asteroid colliding with a black hole."

"I'm sorry?"

"Never mind. Thank you. Can you just keep him there and I'll come down right away?"

"Um, excuse me, Mr. Westerman?" Heather said, timidly interrupting Chuck from his furious wheeling around the store, looking for the woman in the red sundress. "Your wife is back from the beach and on her way down right now."

"That kind of ruins the surprise then, doesn't it?"

"I'm sorry."

"She was right here! Right on this fucking shelf! Is it too much to ask to surprise your wife with a nice present you know she'll like on your last birthday?"

"I—"

"I'm sorry…" he said, taking a deep breath. "Heather, right?" She nodded nervously. "I'm sorry, Heather. I'm not m-mad at you. It's just, well, I'm probably going to die before summer comes. My doctor t-told me I should t-t-take my wife on a nice vacation, but unfortunately, we had to bring my brain tumor along, and it's kind of counter…counter-uh-hhh…" He snapped his fingers frenetically, trying to locate the second part of the word his tumor had devoured.

"Intuitive?"

"Yes! That's it. Isn't the English language a beautiful thing? I wish I could remember it like I used to. You should've seen me play B-B-B-Boggle before I got this damn thing."

"Chuck?" Diana called, walking into the gift shop. She and Heather shared a quick smile of mutual relief that Chuck noticed and resented being the source of.

"I was going to surprise you, but she's not here anymore."

"Are you talking about the Christmas ornament?"

"Yes! The *ornament.*"

"Honey, she's up in the room."

"She is?"

"Yes. Don't you remember I bought her yesterday while you were napping? Then I—I showed her to you when you woke up," Diana said, fighting tears. If only Heather had met the real Chuck Westerman.

"I don't remember any of that," he said like he'd been hideously betrayed by a dear friend.

#

Back in the room, Chuck went down for a nap and had one of those odd, frustrating dreams where everyone in it, including himself, was acting ridiculously out of character. It started out with Chuck alone in a charmless room with fluorescent lights, white walls and a dull gray tiled floor. A single folding chair was placed in the center room, which he found himself sitting in, for some reason, dressed in one of those racing suits NASCAR drivers wear. All of a sudden, Pastor Dave came in holding a racing helmet and wearing a jacket that said CREW CHIEF on the back.

"Dale!" Dave said, looking at Chuck. "You better hurry up! Race starts in two minutes." For some reason, Dave was speaking in a hard-bitten Southern accent, even though he grew up in Nebraska.

"Race?" Chuck asked. "What race? And who's Dale?"

"The Daytona 500 dummy. And what'd'ya mean who's Dale? You're Dale! Dale Earnhardt. The greatest stock car driver to ever walk this earth."

"Don't call me a dummy," Chuck shot back hotly. "Just because I couldn't remember the word *ornament* doesn't mean I'm stupid."

"Ornament? The hell ya talkin' about Dale?"

"I'm not Dale! I'm Chuck, Dave—*Chuck Westerman*. I graduated with honors from Dartmouth! I kick everyone's ass in Boggle! And before I got this tumor, I could remember the word *ornament,* and someday I was going to be the president of a small private college, and I was going to be really good at it! And who knows? After I was done with all that, maybe someday I was going to write the great American novel!"

Dave looked at Chuck like he knew all he was saying was true but, for some reason, derived pleasure from staying committed to this mindless, twisted joke. "We ain't got time for this hogwash Dale. If you don't get off yer ass and go win this race, your tumer's gon' kill ya."

"What are you talking about?"

"You gotta fart in yer brain tumer Dale? Don'tchya remember? The only way that big ole tumer in yer head is gonna go way is if you win the Daytona 500."

"Dave. I'm not Dale Earnhardt. I don't even know how to change the oil in my own car! And besides, I'm the one with the brain tumor, not Dale Earnhardt."

"Sure you are. And sure you do. You gotta mustache don'tchya?" Dave said, as if this erroneous similarity consummated his argument. Just then, a voice called through the PA system, "Gentlemen—start your engines!"

"Better get out there Dale."

At this point, Chuck suspected he was dreaming. Absurd as it all seemed, something in his mind convinced him it was real. That if he went out and won the Daytona 500, his tumor would miraculously disappear. He stood, took the racing helmet from Dave, put it on and walked out of the room to a veritable sea of roaring, faceless people surrounding a huge oval track. Someone on his crew directed him to the number three car, which he climbed into like he'd done it a thousand times. He buckled his seatbelt, turned the ignition and the yellow flag waved. To his surprise, Chuck found that, apparently, he knew everything there was to know about driving a stock car as he took his warmup laps. As the green banner waved, he counted the cars ahead of him—thirteen. He'd passed four of them by the tenth lap. By the twentieth, another five.

He and the car seemed to be one spirit. A flawless, unstoppable tandem of man and machine not to be denied their jug of milk, large shiny cup and brain free of cancer. Rounding the last turn on the thirtieth lap, Chuck glided gracefully past the second-place driver on the inside lane, bearing down on the last car ahead.

Only it wasn't a car! It was a horse! A horse? Yes, of course! A horse!

The number five painted on its strangely familiar rear-end—wait a minute! Chuck had seen that horse before. Hell, he'd ridden it! It was Roy. Roy the bay horse! The only horse he'd ever rode. And atop Roy was none other than Luke Bainbridge. He liked Luke just fine, but right then, he was the only thing standing between Chuck and his happily ever after, and suddenly Chuck couldn't think of anyone in the world he loathed more than the man on the horse in front of him.

His desperate attempts to pass were continually thwarted by Luke and Roy. All his threats to overcome them to that point had been on the inside, but Chuck was a stock-car racing mastermind. The greatest, craftiest, most fearless man behind the wheel to ever walk the planet. He was Dale Earnhardt! He had his rival right where he wanted him. His engine screaming over Luke's left shoulder, pulling him deeper and deeper to the inside, setting him up for Chuck to make his winning move. Over the thundering clamor of the engine, he shouted the very claim he had attempted to refute with Pastor Dave moments before. "I'm Dale Fuckin' Earnhardt!"

On the third turn of the thirty-fourth lap, he made another faux attempt to pass on the inside. His front right bumper inching less than a foot away from Roy's left flank. On the straightaway, he let him pull away a bit, then bore down hot on Roy's heels as they went into turn four. He faked like he was going to pass on the inside again, but as soon as Luke pulled the reins left to block him, Chuck jerked the steering wheel to the right, hammered the clutch, shifted and floored the accelerator…but he'd underestimated the power of the horse and the prowess of its rider. As if Luke had been anticipating this move the whole time, he pulled his reins to the right and gave Roy a swift kick to accelerate with a surprising burst a split second before Chuck did. He pressed the gas the final inch to the floor and kept his line, all-in on his bet as the superior racer. Knowing if he didn't pass Luke now, he never would. Chuck's eyes fixed on Roy's nose. If he could just get past that nose. But Luke played it perfectly. Giving Chuck just enough of a glimpse of the glory ahead, all the while screening him from ever capturing it—Chuck's eyes so fixed on Roy's nose, he forgot about the wall barreling toward him.

Thud!

#

Chuck was roused from the dream by someone opening the bathroom door. Stirring from his side onto his back, his eyes opened to see Diana dressed in an urbane, lipstick-red evening gown. Her freshly bronzed collarbones he'd always found so attractive gleaming against it. Her hair up in a fancy bun, the curls on the sides dangling elegantly against her cheeks—looking as beautiful as the day he'd married her.

"You gotta date?"

"Yes. As a matter of fact, it's my husband's birthday, and I've made us reservations at the restaurant downstairs. There will be an ocean view, wine, and meaningful conversation."

"I don't think your husband packed anything worthy of dining with your stunning presence."

"No, he didn't. It seems all he packed for one of the most beautiful places on Earth was sweatpants and threadbare T-shirts. Lucky for him," she said, walking over to her hanging bag, "his wife always packs for any occasion." Then added, "Something her husband loves about her very much."

She fished out a classic Nantucket-style ensemble from the back of the hanging bag and playfully threw a soft blue button-up and casual khakis over his face.

"He does?" Chuck asked, peeking from under the clothes and raising his eyebrows.

"He better," she shot back with a look. "Otherwise his wife will find someone else to dine with tonight."

"He does!" he said, then rallied out of bed to dress. It had been a while since he'd tucked in a nice shirt. Minus the steroid chub and shaved sides of his head, all-in-all, his tumor felt a little smaller, his sense of dignity a little more apparent.

"That's the man I married," Diana said, appearing over his shoulder in the mirror as he rolled up his sleeves.

"How's my hair?" He grinned.

"Perfect. Do you want your chair?"

His legs were already beginning to tire, but the outfit had dressed up his determination.

"No. It's my birthday."

#

They were shown to their oceanside table on the restaurant patio.

Wine was poured, glasses rang out sweetly in a birthday toast, napkins and conversation unfolded, and Chuck was pleasantly surprised to find his ability to speak had returned to its pre-tumor fluency for an evening.

"So," Diana began, raising her brow. "You're Dale Earnhardt?"

Merlot nearly shot out of Chuck's nose. "*Ah-herm!*" He choked and cleared his throat, then wiped his face with the cloth napkin. "I was, but I crashed into the wall on turn four going two hundred miles per hour, so it looks like I'm just Chuck again."

"Sounds like some dream."

"You could say that. It got me thinking though, you know, about how I'm going to die and all. Obviously, I've been thinking about that for a while, but I guess now I'm gonna say it— Diana…" he said, looking into her hazel eyes. "You have my blessing to remarry after I'm gone. I mean, not just to *anybody*, but someone who will give you and the boys what you deserve. Whether you have to wait ten months or ten years to find him, just know whenever you do, it's what I want for my family."

With welling eyes, Diana took his hand from across the table. "I appreciate that, but we don't have to talk about this right now."

"No. It's okay. I want to. I, uh, actually had someone in mind."

"Okay…" Diana said as she leaned back and took a healthy gulp of wine.

"I was thinking…well, what about James?"

Now it was Diana's turn to snort wine. "James?!?"

"Yeah. *James.*"

"Your cousin, James?"

"Yes!" Chuck said, as she let out a substantial chuckle. "What's wrong with James?"

"Nothing! It's just. I don't ever see myself being in love with him."

"Why not? He's smart, handsome. He's always been good with the boys."

"I know, but it's just—it's just weird. He's your cousin. He's kind of like you, but he's not you."

"That's the idea."

"Honey. It's not the *like you* I object to. It's the *not you*."

"Anyone you marry isn't going to be me."

"I realize that. But if I find someone else, there's a lot of things about you I want them to have. Your compassion, your wit, your passion and drive to help people and be a good person…"

"Not to mention my devilishly good looks."

"Yes," she smiled. "All of that, but to be with someone who has similar mannerisms, who looks a bit like you but isn't, that would just be hard, you know?"

"I suppose I can see your point."

She stretched across the table and kissed his forehead. "Thank you though. For thinking of me. For being willing to talk about this. I don't think it's easy for either of us, but I know it must be especially hard for you."

"Anything for you Dye."

Their server, a pleasant Frenchman named Benoit with a big cut jaw, amazing brown slicked-back hair and a pearly white smile came over to the table with their steaks. Setting their plates in front of them, he took a small bowl off the tray and held it over Chuck's mashed potatoes, then very Frenchly asked, "Would you lyke some…sowah qwueem?"

Chuck stifled a large giggle, then glanced at his wife, who was doing the same. "*Aherm*…Y-Yes, please."

Diana, conscious of her figure, declined Benoit's offer for *sowah qwueem*. When Benoit departed and was finally out of earshot, they burst—not just the laughter they'd been holding in for the last minute, but a release of eight months' tension and grief. They had always had their share of little quarrels, but apart from that, they had always shared laughter. And as they were both aware this might very well be the last time they were together in stitches, they laughed all the more, as if invoking a whole host of angels to join them in their laughing right in the face of grief and its demons…

"So, I have a question for you," Diana resumed when at last, the laughter subsided.

"Ask away dear."

"Looking back on your life, what are you most proud of?"

"You and the boys aside? I guess I'd say I thought our work in Chicago was one of the better investments of my time."

"Yeah?"

"Yeah. Pastoring Calgary has been amazing. It would've been hard to raise a family in inner-city Chicago. But working at La Salle, working with C.Y.C.L.E., teaching those kids to read and write, to love and hope, to problem-solve, to think critically and for themselves. To give them a better shot at finding a meaningful purpose in life and know I was at least doing some small thing to help break the cycle of poverty and liberate the oppressed…I think I could've made for a pretty successful Wall Street lawyer, and to know that I chose walking around in duct-taped shoes and bringing Shakespeare to the youth of Cabrini Green—yeah—I take that to my grave with pride. I'm proud someday you'll be able to tell our boys that."

CHAPTER 14

When Sorrows Like Sea Billows Roll

November 11, 1991—Chugwater, WY ‖

It had been five minutes since Paige parked her walker in front of Haley's door.

The light seeping through the cracks meant Haley was still awake, most likely reading, and yet Paige still hadn't been able to bring herself to knock. Each time she curled her fist to level it against the door, the fallen angel of procrastination appeared before her, exalting persuasive arguments for putting the conversation off until the "right time." A few more days would give her time to come up with the best and least damaging way to say it. Maybe it never needed to be said. Nine-year-olds weren't oblivious. Perhaps they were in matters like keeping track of winter coats and both of their mittens before they went out into the whipping cold November wind to catch the school bus, but Paige had found that most of what children learned from their parents occurred when they weren't even trying to teach them.

In the heavier realms of life, they were ingrained with an incautious wisdom.

In Haley's case, she was aware of the physical deterioration that had afflicted her mother over the last three years and, likely, the grave consequences it implied. To the degree she comprehended the gravity of death, Paige had no idea, but over the past year, her eldest daughter's bright, sapphire eyes had dulled to more of a marbled gray, her brow increasingly furrowed and pensive, to the point it had become as difficult getting Haley out of bed as it was for Paige herself. Most mornings, ten minutes before the bus arrived, Luke opened Haley's bedroom door to find her still furrowed under the covers, futilely attempting to hide from a world she didn't trust would turn out alright. Out of ideas, he'd threatened to pour a cup of cold water on her head more than once, but her mother—feeling guilty her sickness was the source of Haley's brooding bed manner—had persuaded him against the rude awakening. When Haley finally made it to the breakfast table, it was likely she noticed the way her father stared blankly at his All-Bran while her mother remained in bed. When she got home from school, she knew she'd find Paige still there under the covers, sleeping or half-awake, choking down another carrot.

Paige sensed Haley's hope for things turning around had, like her own, been buried deep under the dirt-piled reality of the last three years. Not once had it taken a significant turn for the better. It'd just gotten worse. More bedridden, tear-driven, morphine-stricken. She hadn't walked without her walker in two years, usually opting for the wheelchair over the last nine months.

Most mothers carry a purse. Haley's carried a portable morphine pump.

Yes, some time ago, her oldest daughter had caught sight of death's presence before Paige's door. She could tell by the way she'd catch Haley looking at her each time she pressed the button on her pump. Paige hated that look. That look that said, *I know what you're doing. I know what that button does. I know the more you press that button, the worse things are.*

Haley had never approached her parents with this knowledge. Like her father, she wasn't one to pry into matters where prying was unwanted, but she was a perceptive girl with an acute ability for reading people and situations. Paige wasn't planning to broach the subject of her death with Emma. Her role as the younger sister and less developed notions of mortality absolved her from Paige's sense of obligation to knock on her bedroom door and have this particular conversation. But after her second unsuccessful trip to Germany, a terrible clatter rattled through Paige's conscience as the plane rumbled down the airstrip. Crossing the gloomy expanse of the midnight Atlantic, she knew a terrible, inescapable task awaited her upon landing. In her living will and testament, she must appoint her firstborn daughter to take over as woman of the house at nine years old. For this commission to be voiced by anyone but her own would be iniquitous—a shirking of motherly duties.

Yet how badly she wanted to shirk it.

How desperately she yearned to walk into the bathroom and wash her hands of the plague that would take her life and wreak havoc on those she least wanted havoc to be wreaked. She'd grown to resent her presence in other people's lives. Thirty-nine months unceasingly existing as the tiny blonde elephant in the room. The all-at-once too-fast-and-too-slow ticking time bomb. Desiring, every day, nothing more or less than to die and to live, to no longer be looked upon by human eyes with pain and awkward pity, but dignity and strength…

Thud! Thud! Thud!

"Yes?"

"Haley? Can I come in?"

"You may."

Paige drew a deep breath, turned the knob and shuffled her walker into the room. A cozy and roomy abode with warm-white walls and banana creme carpet. A tall, Pullman-brown bookshelf filled with various children's tales from *Amelia Bedelia* and *The Berenstain Bears* to *Mossflower* and the *American Girls* series.

"You scared me," Haley said as Paige scooted gingerly across the room toward her.

"I did?"

Paige herself had just been thinking the same thing about the nine-year-old girl propped up in the twin-sized bed. Her petite figure had a stately, strangely intimidating presence to it. Placid-blonde curls resting thoughtfully on her shoulders. Giant purple square-rimmed glasses perched prudently on the orbicular Bainbridge nose. Her knees forming a small mountain under the quilt. Her eyes not shying from meeting Paige's like so many others had come to. They locked in with Paige the second she walked in the room, so honest and transparent that all the courage Paige had willed a moment before to knock on the door fled her instantly.

"Yes," Haley said, inserting a bookmark two-thirds of the way through *Martin the Warrior*. "Did you have to knock so loud?"

"I'm sorry dear."

"It's okay."

"Any room for your mom in that bed?"

Haley smiled a fracture, then shifted toward the wall so Paige could lie down next to her.

"Agh," she groaned, easing herself onto the mattress. "Your old mom can't stay on her feet for very long these days, can she?"

"No."

"Does that scare you?"

"Yes. Does it scare you?"

"Yes it does Haley girl," Paige said with welling eyes. Then, taking her daughter's hand and squeezing it tightly, she continued to force the words out. "I wish I could tell you it doesn't, but that would be a lie. It scares me very much."

"I thought so."

"Do you know why it scares me?"

"Sort of…"

"Because someday you're going to grow up to be a beautiful woman. You're going to find some kind, intelligent, handsome, God-loving man like I was lucky enough to find in your dad. And one day you'll put on a pretty white dress and walk down the aisle to marry him, and you're just going to look so beautiful Haley…

"Your grandparents will be there. All your aunts and uncles and cousins and close friends—all the people who love you so much. And your dad will be there to walk you down the aisle…and I'm afraid, because even though all those wonderful people will be there to see you get married—I…I won't be. Not in person at least."

"How do you mean?" Haley asked, also trying to suppress tears.

"Oh Haley girl," Paige said, mustering a smile, "I'll be there…I'll just be watching you from Heaven."

"Because you're going to die?"

"Yes. Everyone's going to die. But I'm afraid for me it's going to come a bit sooner. Quite a bit sooner actually."

"How soon?"

"I don't think I'll be here a year from now…" And as the moment was so bitter any amount of sugar coating wouldn't help, she added, "Likely a lot sooner than that."

Haley buried her face in Paige's chest and began to sob.

"Oh sweetheart…" her mother cooed, stroking Haley's hair and holding her. "I'm sorry. I'm so sorry. I can't even tell you how—this is the hardest thing I've ever had to say to anyone. I love you and your sister so much. It kills me to see you hurt like this."

The muffled words "It's not fair" were sobbed into her breasts.

"I know it's not. It's not fair. You and your sister don't deserve to have to go through this, but you know what?"

"What?"

"Fair or not, life happens. Bad things happen to good people, and good things happen to bad people. But the reason there's still good in the world is because enough good people don't stop being good even when bad things happen. Promise me you won't do that Haley. Promise me you won't use my death as an excuse for treating the people around you badly. As much as I want to stick around to be your mom, what I want even more is for my daughters to love people. After I'm gone, your father's going to have a lot on his plate. I need you to be the woman of the house, okay? I need you to obey him and do exactly what he says because he knows what's best for you, even if you don't feel like he does in the moment. I need you to get out of bed in the morning when he asks you to, and I need you to take care of your sister."

Paige felt the head of tangled blond hair held to her chest nod up and down. "Do you have any questions about all this?"

"Will you sing to me?"

"Of course," Paige said and began to sing the wonderful, pain-riddled anthem of Horatio Spafford's soul. The lyrics written shortly after a three-year period which included the loss of his only son to scarlet fever, the loss of his estate to the Great Chicago Fire, and the loss of his four daughters to a shipwreck crossing the Atlantic to join him in Europe for the holidays. It was this wretched fit of grief, this three-year valley of death and destruction filled to the brim with bitterness and gall, this period of utter unfairness out of which Horatio penned some of the most famous, gorgeous and uplifting words written in the traditional Christian hymnal.

When peace like a river attendeth my way
When sorrows like sea billows roll
Whatever thy lot, thou hast taught me to say
It is well, it is well with my soul

She finished the song and turned off Haley's reading lamp, lying there with her in the dark for a while, stroking her hair until her firstborn fell fast enough asleep. It should've been a comforting moment. The thing had been said. Paige hadn't permitted herself a drop of morphine since the afternoon, wanting to speak to her daughter as the mother she'd been before it—undiluted, strong, coherent. Her focus had been so fixated on the spiritual torment of delivering bad news she'd managed to tune out the screaming pangs of cancer until Haley fell asleep. Her thoughts now went to her pump lying on the nightstand, waiting to offer her dubious relief. As her daughter drew and emitted the long, soothing sounds of her child sleeping in her arms, the flames of mindless pain roared inside her.

Feeling around for her walker through the darkness, she slipped out from Haley's bed as softly as she could. Lifting the tennis balls slightly off the ground and tiptoeing her walker through the blackened room. She turned the knob slowly, then, using all her strength, gripped it tightly and lifted up to keep the hinges from creaking. A trick she'd learned from her older brother Chris when they'd sneak out of the house on summer nights to stargaze in the cornfields.

She walked past her and Luke's bedroom door, the pump she needed lying beyond it on her nightstand. She was tired of numbing her pain. For at least a little longer, she wanted to feel it all in its fullness and reality. Faltering to the couch in the den, she collapsed on her back, looking up through the skylight to the heavens, the same Milky Way she and Chris used to marvel at glistering above the infinite bed of the cornfields. The ceiling in the den was only about seven feet tall, but the skylight peered through a long vertical, four-walled corridor stretching up about fifteen feet. She went back there in her memory—through the skylight to the starlit cornfield just forty miles southeast from where she lay on the couch in the den. Back to the smell of a fresh harvest on a clear night, where she always imagined leaving this earth old and with her loved ones around her, then floating painlessly up into whichever star she pleased. It would start out small at first, just a solitary, shimmering thing, and then all at once, in twenty years and twenty seconds, she'd pass through the great light. Beyond time and space and affliction and evil. And she always imagined that when she finally passed through it, the days that lead up to it would be lived without anger or fear but with acceptance and resolute faith. In this moment, Paige put a pillow over her mouth, screaming festering laments into the art-deco embroidery, weeping as she did.

#

Paige woke in her bed just before eight, with a vague recollection of being carried softly in the strong arms of her husband from the couch in the den to their bed as dawn began to blush through the skylight.

Luke was already in the kitchen forcing down a bowl of All-Bran, fueling up for a long day of feeding cattle in the wind-drifted snow. She resisted the impulse to press the button on her pump and dialed her focus on living two more morphine-free hours of life. It was the clearest her mind had been for months. Knowing once she administered a dose, the gumption to go without it would leave her. If she could just make it a hundred and twenty more throbbing minutes without pressing that damn button, Paige would be as ready to die as she'd ever be under the circumstances she was being asked to do it.

"Luke?" she called. The sound of the dishwasher closing replied, followed shortly by the appearance of her bag-eyed husband in their room.

"Yes dear?"

"I need you to do a few things for me please."

"Okay."

"I need you to bring me the nice set of stationery from the desk and a couple good pens. I'm writing letters to the girls. Four to each of them. There's a piece of jewelry to go with each letter. All the jewelry has been purchased, and I've written all but the last two letters, which will be done by the time you get back from feeding. Sometime this week, I need you to take the letters and jewelry to the bank and put them in our safety deposit box. In my will, you'll find instructions for which jewelry goes with which letter and when specifically the letters are to be given to the girls."

Luke nodded and left the room, returning shortly with the pens and stationery. As he turned to go, Paige grabbed for his fleeting hand and gave it a sturdy squeeze. "Thank you," she said, then pulled him to her lips.

Two toilsome hours later, Paige finished the last two letters to her daughters. They were to be accompanied by a gold ring bearing their respective birthstones, which they were to receive after the birth of their firstborn child. Upon finishing, Paige clicked the top of her pen, then the red button by her waist three times. Everything slowing and clouding as she stuffed and sealed the letters in the envelopes, the last words she'd ever say to her girls.

What words were written upon these hallowed scrawls of paper will remain in the confidence of the characters involved. For they are the secret, sacred words from an ethereal mother to her earthly daughters. A mother who quietly, furiously loved her girls as the Father did His Son.

CHAPTER 15

The Metaphor for the Ripping Apart of Life

May 13, 1991—Cheyenne, WY

Chuck was ready.

At least that was his mindset. Of course, he didn't *feel* ready. He suspected no one—not even Jesus himself—had ever felt truly ready to die, but he remembered someone telling him, "That moment you feel more afraid than ever, that's when you know you're ready..." Who exactly he'd heard this from, and in what context they'd said it, the tumor had besmirched. But over the course of his last days, the words resounded through the ill-stricken sanctuary of his mind like a great cathedral organ.

They'd first come to him on Charlie's first birthday, exactly two months before. He and Diana had attempted to give their youngest as normal and happy a celebration as possible despite their sad, irregular circumstances, inviting every immediate member of the Calgary Baptist family who had been so faithful to their own throughout the last nine months.

The Messners, the Merricks, the Riners, the Levenbaums—they had all come, bringing with them a beautiful, stubborn determination to help give the Westerman family their last seemingly normal day. Parading through the front door in colorful outfits bearing gifts, smiles, cake and hugs of astounding generosity, Chuck recalled how vulnerable he felt letting them into his home when he first started at Calgary Baptist five years ago, wondering if they'd second-guessed their pastoral decision at the sight of *Rolling Stone* magazine's latest issue resting on their minister's coffee table.

Five years later, there they were, with him in his home, and he'd never been more vulnerable or thankful to have them. There was Rick Messner, reminiscing about Brewers great Paul Molitor's thirty-nine-game hitting streak even though he was a Yankees fan. There was Julie Merrick, settling the dispute between Woody and her daughter over who looked like a monkey and smelled like one too. And there was Donna Levenbaum, videotaping the whole shebang.

Then all of a sudden, Diana was cleaning up in the kitchen, Jeremy and Mick were playing in their room, and every guest except for Donna had left. The seemingly normal festivities were over. And there was Donna in his living room, handing him his cowboy hat, ready with the camcorder to shoot Chuck's last recorded words to his youngest son. The son who would only find visual evidence of their personal relationship on a few feet of magnetic tape. His father's face fattened by steroids, his hair and wit thinned by cancer. When it took Chuck's every ounce of strength to hoist Charlie onto his lap to shoot the big scene, the reality that he wouldn't be around for his next birthday or any birthdays following—that within a matter of months, his casket would close at the Cheyenne cemetery with a *thud*, his face never to be looked upon again on this earth—it all hit him like a stone against a tree and he wasn't ready.

Since Hawaii, he felt he'd made a general peace with his death, but the moment his youngest son's head nestled up contently against his heart, he was re-gripped by a fear which burgeoned to anger and told him to fight. Between the rock of his son's skull and the unseen rage now hardening in the chest it was resting on, he wanted to go fist for fist with God. Wanted to knock him to the ground, pin his arms down with his knees and force the Almighty to reason with him.

Had he not given his gifted mind to furthering the kingdom of God? And for it, had he not been compensated with a brain tumor that would leave his wife without a husband? His three sons without a father? If he'd never met Dye, if they'd never met and gone on to conceive three spirited sons, certainly he'd leave more willingly. It was true he'd made a conscious use of his free will to marry Dye, and they'd chosen to have Jeremy and Mick.

But Charlie?

He was the unintended result of a Westerman family Kiawah Island reunion. Of a good bottle of merlot and being made weak in the knees by the poetry and romance of the sand and the waves and the stars and the moon. They didn't think they were conceiving a child who'd never know his father on this earth. They were thinking the whole scene would be made all the more heavenly by a man and his wife making Heaven-sent, contraceptive-free love.

For that, Chuck felt he had a strong case against God to give him more time.

Just enough for Charlie to get a little older so he'd actually remember what it felt like to be told he was loved by his father. After they'd read *The Quiet American* and *Henry V* together and debated their meanings over a beer when he came home from college. After he'd married a wife of noble character and settled into an honorable profession he was passionate about. Once he'd safely crossed the bridge over troubled water, then Chuck would be ready to die.

So he wasn't feeling particularly witty or faithful or brave when Donna asked, "Chuck? Are you ready?" And it was this moment when the strangely familiar voice in his head spoke—*That moment you feel more afraid than ever, that's when you know you're ready.* Chuck nodded to Donna, who pressed the red button. Then he looked down at his son. At his and Diana's little accident sporting his own little cowboy hat, holding the envelope from one of his birthday cards and tearing it in half.

"What d'ya got there, Char? An envelope? Oh! You're gonna tear it in half now huh?" He spiked the camera with a goofy, downcast half-smile and said, "Well…in case you want a metaphor for the striking, ripping apart of life, there it is…" Then, remembering Charlie would see it someday, nipped the ecclesiastical rant in the bud. That was the best he could come up with? *In case you want a metaphor for the striking, ripping apart of life?*

And the whole moment made him realize that what he *really* wanted was to save each of his sons from all this ripping apart of life, but ultimately, no matter what side of Heaven he was on, he wouldn't be able to. They would hurt whether he was there or not. One way or another, their hearts would get broken and broken again. We're all bound to find or be found by trouble. Sooner or later, a bullet will enter the most vital organ of our soul. Whether or not we feel we have it coming is irrelevant. The fact is, you have a bullet in your soul's heart, and the only way through the rest of your life is to remove the little bastard, clean the wound, mend it, then resist the urge to pick at it while time works its healing powers.

And maybe their father's death would teach his sons this most valuable and important lesson at an early age. Maybe when fires came to burn down their childhood home, or beautiful, unsubstantial girls left them with shattered hearts, when their back car window was smashed and their backpack with their computer inside stolen and they lost whole chapters of their hard-written first novel, they'd be savvy veterans in their ability to keep smiling through it. Maybe when Charlie was twenty-four and watched his father look down at one-year-old Charlie and say, "In case you want a metaphor for the striking, ripping apart of life," he'd laugh.

Because it was honest.

Because it was sarcastic.

Because being heroic in the face of cancer must feel anything but heroic. Its glory must be found in the effort to accept its utter ingloriousness. And to truly accept it requires an appropriate number of inappropriate jokes to be made, tears to be wept, obscenities shouted, ecclesiastic comments cynically spoken, hair pulled out, and clothes torn.

Still, Chuck had to come up with something better than *in case you want a metaphor for the striking, ripping apart of life...* If ever there was a father who should have profound last words for his son, it was Chuck. He'd made his living off them. Had spent years huddled over a hot yellow pad—hammering, bending, forging the letters until they transformed into something useful and magnificent. Those who truly mastered the craft were those who learned to hold their ten-ton tongue until they truly had a thousand-pound thing to say. For the art of writing was not in speaking but listening. Yet even then, Chuck heard no great speech or profound wisdom scribbling sentences in his cranium. The moments of triumph were what kept the writer writing. Few feelings were more satisfying than bringing order to the chaos of the mind. But some were too tremendous and overwhelming to be conquered with words. Reaching the peak of psychological mountains required climbing them, and Chuck found that most days, it was a humbling endeavor. Some days, the weather of life was more powerful than his determination to summit. Sometimes all he could do was accept his inadequacies, return to base, take refuge in the warmth of his campfire, and try again the next day. Though in Chuck's case, there wouldn't be a next day, and so all he could do was cradle his son in his lap and sing Sinatra to him while he had the chance.

"Alright Charlie..." Chuck said, getting his attention. "Are you ready?" Charlie looked up at him curiously as he began to sing, *Start spreading the news*…a smile spreading across his son's face. *I'm leavin' today*…and nine months ago, he would've been able to sing the whole song word for word. Yet even now, in this sacred moment, the golf ball-sized Satan in his brain was trying to ruin it. The only lines the ruthless prick hadn't been able to destroy being the first and last, and all Chuck could do was accept it and sing what he knew.

> *In old New York*
> *And if I can make it there*
> *I'm gonna make it anywhere*
> *It's!*
> *Up!*
> *To!*
> *You!*
> *New York!*
> *New York!*

At the conclusion of the rendition, Chuck imitated the applause of a Broadway crowd, causing the dimples Charlie was already wearing to double in size. Chuck looked into his eyes, reciprocating the smile. "We make a great duo—you and me. The two of us should go on Broadway." At this suggestion, Charlie let out an incomprehensible exclamation. "Do you want to? Do you think we could make it?" He started bouncing wildly in Chuck's lap. "It's worth a try anyway." Charlie removed his cowboy hat and pointed to the one Chuck was wearing. "You want to trade?" Chuck said with a laugh. Charlie held out his hand to accept, and they made the exchange. Chuck put on his new hat, then helped Charlie with his. "There you go. Yes. The big hats are very fashionable. The little hats might not be you."

It then occurred to Chuck that while Charlie would never get the opportunity to remember hearing his father say he loved him in person, he could at least give him the benefit of hearing it through the miraculous, time-transcending medium of the home videotape. "Charlie, I want you to know that—oh…" Again, Charlie had taken his hat off, a shit-eating grin on his face as he held it up to Chuck. "You want yours back now huh?" This newly invented game of incessant hat-swapping went on for a while, Charlie laughing hysterically each time they did, almost as if he was attempting to thwart Chuck's efforts to assume a more serious tone and say what was on his mind. As if he knew once he delivered that climactic and incredibly crucial line for a son to hear from his father, it would be curtains for the only scene he'd ever know of their relationship in this world. Chuck looked at Donna. "I think if it was up to Charlie, this would go on forever." Taking the cue, she secured the camera on the tripod and walked over to the recliner while Chuck commandeered both hats and handed them to her. She hid them out of sight, and Charlie started to whine, Chuck bouncing him patiently on his knee until the fit subsided…

Craning his neck, Chuck kissed the crest of his youngest's sweet-smelling head. "I love you Charlie."

#

Two months later, Charles Beck Westerman found himself in the same hospital where Charles MacDuff Westerman had been born fourteen months to the day before. In the same red brick building where he arrived in the world in Cheyenne, his father was about to meet Heaven. They brought along his record player for his last stay at CRMC, and as the needle channeled the melodies of Sinatra swimmingly through the spinning vinyl grooves, he wondered if someday Charlie would laugh when he watched his father say, "In case you want a metaphor for the striking, ripping apart of life…"

As "It's Up to You, New York" came through the speakers, his dejected organs began to shut down. His body went into panic. His chest tightened, lungs gasped, muscles convulsed. But the soul of Chuck Westerman experienced a peace passing understanding. All his willed feelings of hope over the last eleven months now took a natural form in his brain. As his suffering came to a conclusion, he could finally take consolation in knowing he'd fought to the end. That his fight in this world was over, and despite losing some of the battles, he now interpreted this feeling as a kind of Holy Ghost telling him he'd won the war.

Yes. That brief, cynical, Jeremiah-like lament would make Chuck more human to his son. More genuine and courageous. Those who truly possess faith acknowledged their doubt but don't subscribe to it. One has to permit little moments of imperfect humanity in the midst of tribulations, gather themselves, then redouble their efforts to go on living with a superhuman mindset. That small, dark instant wouldn't overshadow the abundance of hope and faith which had marked the last chapter of Chuck's life but made it shine even brighter. The light that beckoned those who knew him to say—cliche as it sounds—that his last two months on this physical earth were his spiritual best. That on his deathbed, he was still cracking jokes, still spreading joy, still trying to remind people how seriously important it was to smile. And someday his sons would hear how he'd remained faithful to his God, that he'd breathed his last with a divine confidence God would remain faithful to them after he was gone …

As the song wound down, the rhythmic measures of Chuck's heart graph grew sporadic and illogical, but he focused his last breaths on Sinatra. He'd passed through the flames of feeling more afraid than ever. His cowardice had been consumed by them, and he'd been refined with a courage as pure and bold as good music. Breathing his last, he didn't perceive the rhythmless *beep…beep-beep…beep…beep-beep-beep-beep-beep-beep-beep!*

What he heard were the last words he ever sang to his last-born son.

In old New York—*beep!*—And If I can make it there—*beep!*—I can make it anywhere—*beep!*—It's up to you—*beep!*—New—*beep!*—York—*beep!*—New—*beep!*—York!

Beeeeeeeeeeeeeeeeeeeeeeeeeeeeeeeeeeeeeeeep!

The nurses came in as the last song on the B-side finished. And as they pulled the white sheet over Chuck Westerman's face, the sound coming through the needle died, rose, and came to life again.

CHAPTER 16

Holes in His Feet

May 13, 1991—West Allis, WI ‖

Aaron was barefoot when he got the call.

After seven years, his favorite wrestling shoes had finally crapped out on him, so he'd bought a pair of new Asics the closest he could find to the old ones. Seven years later, he'd forgotten how much of a pain in the ass buying and breaking in new shoes was for someone in his position…

Transfer into the pickup. Remove the wheels. Heave it all up into the passenger seat. Drive to the mall. Unload the chair. Re-attach the wheels. Transfer out. Wheel half a goddamn mile through the mall to the shoe store. Deal with Nick-the-nervous-nineteen-year-old-shoe-boy who seemed about as comfortable helping an incomplete-quadriplegic as a fundamentalist Wisconsin Christian would a trans-woman wearing a Chicago Bears scarf to hide their Adam's apple. Aaron needed a good pair that would fit his needs and last another seven years, which weren't cheap, which meant as Nervous Nick ran Aaron's card, he had more murderous thoughts about his kindly but miserly tenant Shakey Kwiatkowski, who was, yet again, late paying rent.

Then…wheel *back* half a damn mile through the mall.

Transfer in. Remove wheels. Heave chair over lap to passenger seat. Drive back home. Unload chair. Reattach wheels. Transfer out.

From the time he left his apartment to the time he got back, almost four hours had passed. This was only the time it took to buy them, but it was all Aaron had in him to accomplish that Sunday. Most of Monday would be spent sewing on heel loops and cutting holes in the bottom. His old pair had come with loops, but his new pair didn't, so he'd have to tack some on with Bea's old sowing machine.

It was the constant conundrum of Aaron's life—almost every basic task people with abled bodies tackled took him twice to five times as long, leaving him with considerably less amount of time to actually make a living. Sure, he could restore a vintage Studebaker motorcycle as well as anyone, but the time cost of labor didn't yield enough in the way of profit to allow him to prosper. Most days, it felt as if everything in his world suffered paralysis. Not just in the physical, but the disabling effect that rippled through every aspect of his life post-*splash*. His body relied on almost all of his mental resources to function, and so his mental resources were largely inhibited from being put to use for other pursuits because it was constantly working on solving problems like figuring out how to sew loops on the heels of his shoes with limited dexterity. Before he jumped into Lake Joanis, his plan had never included being a landlord. The *plan* was to callous his hands doing something other than pushing two wheels from A to B. He would've made a hell of an honest mechanic.

So there he was, sitting barefoot in his chair, wearing his favorite Levi's and Earnhardt T-shirt with Dale's head printed on the back—racer's ball cap, pilot's aviators, coroner's mustache. And Aaron thinking his most frequent thought—*I didn't sign up for this shit*—as he cut holes in the bottom of his shoes to ease the pain of slow-resolving pressure sores whilst simultaneously trying not to slice his hand open and so open a different, slow-resolving wound. At this moment, the phone rang with a perspiring portentousness that gave his fifth vertebrae a split-second of hot, terrible feeling back, which left him as quickly as it came.

He knew who was calling and what she was calling to tell him before he lifted the phone off the dial. When you'd lost as many things as Aaron, you developed the cursed gift of harrowed clairvoyance. It came suddenly, and it didn't matter if it was June or January. When it came, the air around him instantly turned sultry and choked like it was that last fateful day of summer 1973.

"Son of a bitch," he said, pulling away the shirt sticking to his sweat-drenched chest, then finally picked up the phone. "Hello?" Just as he'd forebode, it was Diana calling to say, "Chuck's gone home." This phrasing, "Chuck's gone home," for *your brother-in-law is dead*, solicited a confusing set of simultaneous reactions in Aaron's head. His love for his sister wanted to say something that would hold her in Cheyenne from his apartment in West Allis. His disdain for her delivering this news using the diction of a doctrine he didn't subscribe to made him want to reply, "No Dye. He's just gone."

And then there was the other part of him that loved and respected Chuck. That actually believed if any pastor merited a ticket to an imaginary heaven, it was his brother-in-law. Chuck had never attempted to bulldog him into a conversion to Christianity, had never tried to bait a conversation, attempting to catch Aaron like a twenty-pound trophy bass he could hold up for Jesus to gain admittance through the pearly gates. He'd always treated Aaron like a person he respected, not a fish he was trying to stuff and mount on his saintly wall. Now Aaron couldn't help but wonder if perhaps his brother-in-law wasn't just a very unfortunately mistaken brainiac…which meant maybe Diana was right. Maybe Chuck *had* gone home, which at that moment would've been a great comfort to Aaron and, come to think of it, shed a soothing ray of hope on all the losses he'd suffered in his life. It would mean someday he might walk, jump, swim again. Would again be able to go hunting with his father and finally have sex on top for once.

But why go through any of that shit at all? Why did he ever have to lose his legs? Why did Chuck have to lose his brain, his life? His sister, her husband. His nephews, their father. He told Diana he was sorry, which felt grossly inadequate, but he couldn't think of anything else to say. They'd barely hung up when the phone rang again. He'd bet his good remaining vertebrae it was his mother. Calling frantically to ask all the unsettling questions rumbling in his mind out loud. Could Dye—the woman who sometimes cried just because it was January—could *she* get through this? Would she ever find someone as good as Chuck again? Would the boys turn out okay?

He didn't want to hear these questions asked aloud. Come to think of it, he couldn't sit another goddamn second in the Godforsaken apartment he'd lived in too long five years ago. Grabbing his truck keys, Aaron left his mother to ring, the new hole-less shoes to sit on his workbench and wheeled out the door without bothering to lock up.

#

Shakey Kwiatkowski had just trickled out of bed to let the eleven o'clock sunlight into his second-floor apartment. A benevolent, lazy man and a hippie before the term was coined, Shakey opened the blinds to see Aaron wheeling acrimoniously toward his Chevy S-10, which reminded Shakey he was, again, three days late paying rent, which, by Shakey's clock, meant he had a week before he needed to think about paying it.

He often watched Aaron get into his pickup from the bedroom window as he smoked his morning doobie. A quadriplegic landlord and a second-floor apartment with no elevator was the reason he'd signed the lease in the first place. A combination that relieved his paranoia of a proprietor popping into his place during his midmorning blaze. Besides, the first time Shakey met his landlord was in Aaron's apartment, and he didn't exactly give off the vibe of someone who thumbed his nose at the smell of Hindu Kush or, more importantly, called the cops. Even sitting in his wheelchair, Aaron looked tall. Shakey guessed that, standing, he measured around six-three, but there he sat—a dignified maverick, shirtless, with long, tangled sun-blond hair and discerning brown eyes. His caved chest bearing a tattoo of a young, topless Native American woman standing in a posture of untamed serenity. A noble and rebellious smile light on her beautiful face, her breasts unburdened, her eyes a little sad in that way that made you want to hold her. She looked real, and even as Aaron sat still, Shakey swore he saw her blue-green eyes shift once or twice. Admittedly, he was pretty baked, but still, he liked to imagine his eyes hadn't been deceived and that, in some other world, she was alive and just as lovely.

But when he signed the lease, Shakey hadn't anticipated

the added perk of watching Aaron perform his pickup transfers. He took pride in being the kind of person who truly appreciated the will and aptitude his landlord employed to accomplish what, for most people, was a simple act. Without the joint, he wondered if he would've ever recognized the poetry of Aaron's every precise and calculated move. His mastery of the struggle for position and leverage. A holy moment stoned old Shakey noticed while everyone else was too busy and wrapped up in their own world to take note of life's subtle, broken beauties. At some point, he got the idea to start timing Aaron's transfers, starting from the moment he opened the driver's door and stopping once he got in and shut it. Usually, it took about four minutes, but once he'd clocked Aaron at two and a half. That day also happened to be the closest Shakey had ever seen him come to falling off his transfer board.

Today, as he watched Aaron, it was apparent through the window something was bothering him. For one thing, he was barefoot, which, although Shakey couldn't think of a reason why someone in Aaron's shoes would necessarily need, well, shoes, it seemed notable that today was the only time he'd observed his landlord not wearing them.

The darkness of Aaron's day became even more apparent in the physical nature of his transfer. Not that it was sloppy. In fact, it was as flawless as Shakey had ever witnessed, yet done with an impatience even more reckless than the day Aaron nearly fell off the transfer board. His normally stolid face looked distraught, and Shakey's aging eyes even thought they caught a glimpse of a tear drooping down Aaron's cheek. His maneuvers making the transfer were angrier, swifter, not as tranquil for snoopers like Shakey to find comfort in. At two minutes and fifteen seconds, Aaron was in the driver's seat, slamming his pickup door shut, accompanied by an obscenity yelled loud enough for Shakey to hear through the closed window.

Usually, it was against Shakey's principles to do anything practical after smoking his morning doobie, but today he would make an exception. Stubbing out his joint in the ashtray, saving the roach for later, he floated to the living room and opened the top drawer of his desk. After much rummaging, at last, he came up with his checkbook.

#

"Fuck!" Aaron thundered, slamming the door of his black Chevy S-10. Igniting the engine, the cassette in the tape player picked up where it had left off in the middle of John Prine's "Paradise."

> *When I die let my ashes float down the Green River*
> *Let my soul roll on up to the Rochester dam*
> *I'll be halfway to Heaven with Paradise waitin'*
> *Just five miles away from wherever I am*

The first time he took a liking to John Prine was when Chuck and Dye lived with him in West Allis. He'd heard a couple of Prine's songs before that, quickly dismissing him as a Kentucky bumpkin based on his sound before actually listening to the lyrics. One night after Chuck and Aaron got done watching *SNL* and came to the end of a six-pack, Chuck said he was going to join Diana, who'd gone to bed forty-five minutes earlier after Alicia left.

"Bullshit! There's still another six-pack in the fridge. You can't go to bed until you help me finish it off."

"It's late. Dye and I have to get up early tomorrow and

make it to Chicago by ten to catch the service at La Salle."

"She can drive, and you can grow a pair. Tell her I kicked your ass and wouldn't let you go to bed until you helped me kill off the rest of the beer."

"That wouldn't be a half-bad excuse if your ass was physically capable of kicking mine."

"Oh c'mon Charles! Let's get so drunk I can't walk."

"I'll make you a deal. I'll stay up with you under two conditions. First, I only have to drink two beers. You can do whatever you want with the other four."

"I actually like that better than the original proposal. You've got yourself a—"

"Second—you have to listen, I mean actually *listen*, to three John Prine songs with me."

Aaron had been giving Chuck a lot of flak about his love for John Prine ever since he inserted his first album in Aaron's cassette player on their way to a Brewers game. Since that day, whenever Chuck put him on the record player in the apartment, Aaron would wheel into the room singing made-up bumpkin-ish lyrics in a nasally country twang and plucking an air guitar with yokel-ish mannerisms…

"Son of a—" Aaron rolled his eyes. "Why? Chuck, *why* do you insist on making me listen to this backcountry blowhard?"

"Because that's where his brilliance lies. See, he *sounds* like a country bumpkin, but he writes songs like a musical genius. It's high art the commoner can understand. That's what most people don't get about Shakespeare. They think he's only for stuffy Ivy League WASPs like myself because the language is difficult for us to understand. But in his day, that's how people spoke. One minute he's pondering the human condition—the next, he's making a joke about French people having syphilis. And who went to his plays? Everyone from the Falstaffs of London on up to Queen Elizabeth."

"First off, you are one goofy bastard. Second, I stopped listening when you said Shakespeare."

"C'mon! Three songs. And then we can talk about whatever you like until I finish my beers."

"Alright, but I'm not going to enjoy it."

"We shall see."

Knowing his audience, Chuck started off with "Illegal Smile." The chorus of which rang—

> *And you may see me tonight with an illegal smile*
> *It don't cost very much but it lasts a long while*
> *Won't you please tell the man I didn't kill anyone*
> *No I'm just tryin' to have me some fun*

Aaron hadn't smoked pot for years, but Chuck figured it would help combat his brother-in-law's stigmatism about Prine being a redneck. Plus, he figured quick-witted Aaron would start to open his heart to John Prine when he heard the line in the first verse that went *bowl of oatmeal tried to stare me down, and won*...his prediction was correct. The words *and won* were sung, and Aaron broke into a reluctant chuckle.

As the song finished with *No I'm just tryin' to have me some fun, well done, hot dog bun, my sister's a nun,* Aaron let out a full-bellied, "Ha!" And Chuck knew by the end of their listening, he'd make a believer out of his brother-in-law. He followed with "Your Flag Decal Won't Get You into Heaven Anymore," prefacing it with one of the few times Aaron ever heard him talk about his faith.

"As an aspiring man of the cloth, I hope to someday

deliver a sermon based on this next song. Despite what many people think, Jesus doesn't consider the word *Republican* to be synonymous with *Christian*. And I know this isn't much of a concern for you, but if you'll humor me…"

"Preach it, preacher!" Aaron egged him on. He enjoyed prodding Chuck when he got fired up.

"But it's that kind of Pharisaic bullshit thinking that makes me want to be a pastor! And it's not because I voted for Carter, but because my faith comes before my politics, and it doesn't matter if you're left or right—what matters is your relationship with Jesus."

"Amen! Now play the song because I have no idea how that relates to John Prine."

Chuck adjusted the needle to the seventh track, and again, Aaron rewarded him with a smile as he heard the chorus.

> *But your flag decal won't get you into Heaven anymore*
> *They're already overcrowded from your dirty little war*
> *Now Jesus don't like killin' no matter what the reason's*
> * for*
> *And your flag decal won't get you into Heaven any-*
> * more*

"This is the worst…" Aaron chuckled as the song ended. "What kind of Hell do you have in store for me next?"

"'Paradise,'" Chuck replied and brought the needle back to number five—*I'll be halfway to Heaven with Paradise waitin' / Just five miles away from wherever I am.*

#

"Are you serious?" Aaron screamed as "Paradise" played and he slammed the gearshift from reverse to drive. Punching the eject button on his cassette player, he yanked the tape out of the deck, throwing it against the passenger seat floorboard. A rash decision he immediately regretted when he noticed a hairline fracture in the plastic shell. Squeezing the gas throttle with his right hand, he tore out of the parking lot, not knowing where he was headed, just that he needed to drive for a while. His psyche led him south on I-94 toward Chicago. The trees adjacent to the interstate flashing, then fading in the rearview like the old happy memories of weekend drives to the Windy City to see Chuck, Dye and his nephews.

At least he could still drive. Almost every other one of life's able-bodied liberties he'd been stripped of, their thrills and elations he could no longer recall, but driving was one of his last remaining semblances of joy and freedom. He couldn't really remember what it felt like to swim, to walk, to build something with his own two completely functional hands, but he could still drive, and when he did, he could still feel a little of his old youth pumping in the blood.

Halfway to Chicago, Aaron was still forlorn, but turning the corner onto a smoother stretch of grief. He got off at an exit around Green Oaks and pulled into a vacant parking lot to empty his leg bag. A little after noon, the first swelters of mid-spring radiated from the asphalt. Leaning down, he grabbed the cassette off the floorboard to inspect the damage. The plastic was fractured, but on the whole, the tape looked like it would still function. Inserting it in the cassette deck, John Prine picked up where he left off at the end of "Paradise." As Aaron accelerated up the ramp onto I-94 headed north back to his apartment, he swore he heard his brother-in-law's voice singing "Pretty Good" with Prine through the fuzzy speakers—

Moonlight makes me dizzy
Sunlight makes me clean
Your light is the sweetest thing
That this boy has ever seen

He decided to loop around through Waukesha to get back to West Allis. Over the course of the last couple hours, the afternoon heat had ascended from the mid-60s to the high-80s. He drove past the house he and Dye grew up in, the swimming pool at the country club, and even their old church, wondering what life would've been like had they never moved to Stevens Points the summer after Diana graduated high school. He kept on wondering that as he meandered slowly back to West Allis. When he finally pulled into the lot of his apartment, the drive had lasted long enough for "Pretty Good" to come back around on the tape. Aaron started questioning if he'd always sung one of the lines wrong because he swore this time, Prine sang—

Moonlight makes me dizzy
Sunlight burns my feet

"Wait? Is it *sunlight makes me clean* or *sunlight burns my feet?*" Aaron wondered as he threw the gear shift in park and felt his shirt sticking to his chest.

God it was hot.

He looked down at his feet—cooking against the black rubber floor mat like brats on a Weber grill. "For fuck's sake!" he shouted, picking his blistered feet off the floor to inspect the damage. It was bad. Catastrophic in Aaron's world. He'd violated his golden rule—he'd compounded the problem. Physically and psychologically, the coming months had, in a day, become significantly more treacherous than they'd normally be, and normal for Aaron was no picnic.

#

When he finally got home from the hospital late that night, Aaron found an envelope that had been shoved under his door. Inside was a little yellow note with a check. It was Shakey Kwiatowski's rent, plus an extra fifty dollars—about the amount Aaron paid for his new Asics.

Sorry I'm late again. Here's a little extra for your patience —Shakey

CHAPTER 17

Measures on a Heart Graph

December 21, 1991—I-25 between Cheyenne and Chugwater, WY

Forty months.

Forty days in the desert without food was a long time, but forty months of watching the only woman he'd ever loved suffer through bone-cindering cancer? Luke was losing patience for the angels to arrive and attend to him. He'd just taken Paige to CRMC for what the doctors told him would be the last time. Over the last forty months, he'd pictured this moment coming with some semblance of relief.

It didn't.

Luke saw no halos on the pitch-black horizon as he drove home north on I-25—his green GMC single cab pickup climbing and descending the plains' broad swells like measures on a heart graph. The distant, pulsing lights of satellite towers and occasional faint flickers from country homes proclaiming the birth of Christ only reminded him of hospital monitors. Of the handful of southbound cars he passed, three of them forgot to turn off their brights. Luke stared blankly through them, imagining the moment Paige would pass through the great light.

A barrage of further battering thoughts ensued—the realization that he'd seen Paige on the ranch for the last time. Never again would he walk in after a long day of feeding steers and doctoring water bellies to the smell of her chicken tortilla casserole or her rhubarb pie. She made a great rhubarb pie. Maybe even better than his mother, who he always thought would own the block on rhubarb pie. Never again would Paige sleep by his side or play carols on the piano while he wrote his annual Christmas story at the desk across the den. She hadn't done most of those things in a long time, but something about her not even being there eating carrots by the bushel made the gravity of it all hit him all at once.

The 1200-day tidal wave of his wife's deterioration would finally topple, but the riptides of absence and grief were already pulling him under and thrashing him against the coral. Furthermore, these soul fractures were compounded by the feeling that he shouldn't feel them. That he should be able to take solace in his wife finally nearing the conclusion of her anguish. "Lord…" Luke began to pray, then flat-lined. What he really wanted to say, God didn't want to hear. If only God would leave him alone for a while. Give him a weekend to curse his name and be brazen in his anger—maybe then he'd feel like praying nice. But God was always near, silent and relentless, listening to his every thought, monitoring his every move.

At seventy-five miles per hour, Luke was permitting himself the full expedience of Wyoming state law but violating the self-governed sixty-five he usually kept on the principles of patience, prudence, fuel economy and good stewardship. Halfway way back to the ranch, his thoughts barreling through the prairie night abyss at reckless speeds, he signaled his blinker for Exit 29, eighteen miles before the turnoff for the house. He stopped at the top of the ramp, put the gearstick in neutral and strangled the steering wheel, lowering his forehead against the hub of the wheel as he wept in great soundless tremors.

Somewhere in the last forty months, he'd forced himself to stop feeling anything. Like he'd hooked himself up to some kind of emotional morphine drip. The tears dripping down on the hay-crumbed floor of the pickup awakened his sense of humanity. A reminder he was alive in the world. That his sorrow sprang from a pure and honest place—those white-knuckled wells of disappointment, deep-seated in the pastures of the human heart. Where the forage for meaning, the labors of love, and the endless and tiresome struggle for peace reside. Luke flexed his cheeks tightly, jamming his brow against the hub of the wheel.

Beeeeeeeeeep! Beeeeeeeeeep! Beeeeeeeeeep! Beeeeeeeeeeeeeeeeeeeeeeeeeeeeeep!

The shout of a different horn sounded behind him. In his rearview, a brown hatchback impatiently flashed its brights. He put the pickup back in gear and slowly accelerated down the ramp, reentering the highway and maintaining a steady speed of sixty-five the rest of the way home.

#

The pickup rumbled over the cattle guard a little after eleven.

Luke parked in the driveway and went to enter the house through the garage before nearly tripping over a large box propped against the door. Flicking on the lights, he looked down to see the electric train set someone donated to Chugwater First Baptist Church for the annual Christmas drive. To be given, as the yellow post-it note stuck to the box reminded him, *To a family in need.*

He nearly cried again.

Someone must've noticed the girls eyeing it in the basement during the potluck. Maybe they'd pictured the Bainbridge household on Christmas morning 1991—the prior traditions tainted, the noticeable silences unfilled, the laughs left unfinished in the absence of the family matriarch. Maybe they'd realized Christmas shopping had never been high on Luke's to-do list, especially not this year. He wasn't big on lavishing his children with gifts they'd tire of in a month. Once they assembled the tracks and watched the battery-powered train go around a few times, how much fun was left to be had? Not enough to justify the price tag. It left little room for the imagination and cluttered the storage closet. But he supposed this year, the four hours of distracted relief it would bring his daughters was worth the price of consumerism.

He picked the box up and walked back around the house to the shop. A tall, four-cornered structure with an A-framed roof, fastened to a concrete foundation and enclosed by large sheets of ribbed steel the color of elephant skin. Luke could never decide if it was more of a shop or a barn, so he'd settled on simply calling it the Steel Building. The sliding doors stood all the way up to the chin of the roof, made of the same ribbed steel as the rest of the building, only painted white. Luke set the train down, grabbed a door handle with each hand, and performed a sort of reverse chest fly, snapping his elbows to full extension as momentum carried the doors to the end of the tracks. The wind howling through the gap-toothed entry like a lonely coyote. The thin, steel ribs rippling from the inside out.

Re-gathering the box, he stepped in and flipped the light switch.

Luke's office said a lot about the kind of rancher he was. Thoughtful, efficient, tidy to the point of practicality before crossing the threshold to unnecessarily anal. He'd built a stable in the southeast corner for Roy and Biv, where a smaller, hinged door opened into the corral. In the northeast corner, he kept an emergency supply of small, square-baled hay. The tractor was parked between the stables and the haystack, the ATV parked parallel behind the tractor—this comprised the east half of the building. His workbench was sandwiched between the stable and the sawbuck he'd built to cradle retired fenceposts while he quartered them into firewood. Six feet from the sawbuck was the wood stack, which doubled to enclose his work area like a sort of rancher's cubicle. The north wall held all the various tools and materials needed to keep his operation running—rolls of bailing twine, wire barbed and barbless, bungee cords, towing chains, wire stretchers, a steel post pounder, a set of posthole diggers, wire brushes, various ropes and pulleys for pulling windmills, a grease gun, sandbags, pointed and flat-nosed shovels, scoop shovels, pitchforks, shop brooms, spare corral boards and two self-standing eight-foot basketball hoops.

He purchased the hoops the previous fall when Haley started third grade. The largest town in the county was Wheatland, about thirty-five hundred people, located twenty-five miles north on the interstate from Chugwater—population 192. They had a rec league for third-and fourth-graders, and Luke negotiated with the director to start a team in Chugwater, barring him coming up with a suitable solution for meeting the league's eight-foot-basket requirements.

In Cheyenne, he found two baskets with fiberglass backboards and breakaway rims, then took them up to Jim

Collins in Wheatland. On a thin, circular steel base, Jim mounted two vertical poles, welding them together with a crossbar to resemble a tall, slender H. The backboards were mounted to the uprights of the H, with another pole braced diagonally from the crossbar to the back of the circular base. The brace not only served to make the framework sturdier but also discouraged ambitious eight-year-olds from trying to run (or dribble) between the uprights.

Luke walked slowly to the northeast corner of the building, inspecting the box displaying the plastic train set and shaking his head as he tucked it in the dark cranny between the haystack and the wall. Toy companies—trying to reinvent the wheel of childhood elation all in the name of annual profit increase (batteries sold separately). Months of his own youth had been spent in front of the hoop his father had bolted to the garage for his oldest brother Joe's thirteenth birthday. Luke was five then, his middle brother Andrew eleven, giving him a considerably longer career to own the record for most field goals made on the driveway hoop among the Bainbridge brothers. It took him the better part of an afternoon to gun his first shot in from the hip, the ball depositing through the chain net with a chime like money in a cash register. When it was too cold or windy to shoot outside, he played in the basement using a tennis ball and a hollowed-out-Jiffy-Pop-handle tin rim, which was where he invented the game he'd later adapt to the driveway. The game that would always keep the practice of shooting as something to be enjoyed rather than labored at and that would play a large role in his development as the mainstay of the championship-contending 1970 Albin Wildcats going into his senior year.

The game was to pick two college teams, say Syracuse

versus Kansas. Then he'd pick a spot on the court, say a ten-footer from the baseline, and Syracuse would shoot from that spot. If it went in, the 'Cuse went up two-zero. If the shot missed, they got one more shot from that same spot, this time worth one point. Then Kansas was given the same opportunity from that spot. Up to two shots, the first worth two, the second worth one.

Each team was given fifty possessions, and by the end of the game, Luke had attempted somewhere around one hundred fifty field goals from various spots on the court. He'd play out entire tournament brackets over the course of a weekend. Announcing the play-by-play as he practiced shot-faking and pulling up from the elbow. Hearing the roar of the imaginary crowd when he kissed in a fifteen-footer off the glass.

As he got older, his shot conformed to the fundamentals of the game. Keeping his elbow in, emphasizing the hand-in-the-cookie-jar follow-through, using the backboard when it was to his angular advantage. He never understood people who didn't use the glass because it lacked aesthetic grandeur. The beauty of the game was that getting the ball through the cylinder was worth two points, no matter how you got it there. It was an irrefutable law of the round ball—the more open and proximal shots you take, the more you get squared up to the basket with your feet set, the better your chances of scoring. By the time he entered his senior year, no player in Wyoming Class-B basketball was more deadly from twelve-to-fifteen feet on the wing. He perfected the art in the driveway—dialing in on the top corner of the square, elbow in, follow through...*bank, swish!*

Seven times out of ten—elbow in, follow through... *bank, swish!*

There was something already in the spot where he was trying to stash the train set. Peering in the dark crevice, he found the ball his father gave him for his fifteenth birthday. The leather scuffed and faded but still holding air like the lungs of a deep-sea diver. Kirk Bainbridge didn't give many gifts, but when he did, it was always useful, with intention and built to last.

Luke dribbled once, twice, then took aim at one of the eight-foot hoops...*bank, swish!*

Feeding would come early tomorrow, and should the six-to-twelve inches of snow the weatherman had predicted fall overnight, it wouldn't be a particularly easy day of it. There was also a gate he needed to re-brace, but he wasn't ready to go in just yet and look at that bed. His wife not in it and never to be again. He pulled one of the baskets front and center to the open floor of the Steel Building, warming up with twenty brooding free throws, trying arduously to resonate how the man shooting the ball now could be the same as the one who'd last shot around with the same ball at a park in British Columbia nine years before. It was the fall before Haley was born, the year he and Paige lived in East Vancouver doing college ministry for InterVarsity Christian Fellowship.

Growing up in Albin, he'd spent his college days and early twenties in Laramie working for InterVarsity Christian Fellowship and calling local high school sports for KOWB. Things were good in those days. He loved his wife, found purpose and enjoyment in his work, and apart from the large tree that fell through the roof of their apartment one particularly windy night, the years generally went by free of any significant hardships. Then one day, he woke to an inexplicable restlessness flittering in his chest. Each subsequent morning it seemed to grow a little more until, eventually, it came to dominate his sense of equanimity. He could find no obvious reason for his suddenly disgruntled state other than a hankering for a change of scenery.

One gorgeous June afternoon driving back to the ranch for the weekend to help his father pull a mill, he gazed out across the land he knew and loved better than any in the world. The land that had provided him a happy childhood. That still sea of prairie he'd always found solace in. The pastures thick and luscious with green grass, the wildflowers constellating them with color. The cattle contently chewing their cud. Their smooth, shiny black and red coats a sign of good health and the promise of a bountiful year for the Hodge & Bainbridge Livestock Company. And maybe if it was late January, when the pastures were brown and beaten and the visual evidence of a stiff wind bent the scarce, pale, brittle grasses as if calling for the spirit's submission to the daunting task of persevering through winter—maybe if Luke looked out at *that* prairie and didn't find his usual solace, he wouldn't have given the feeling significant consideration. But in June, Wyoming was garbed in her most beautiful spring dress. It was this view that made him recall his love for her even in January, knowing her current depravity would make her coming abundance that much sweeter.

Delay had a way of inducing a grateful heart.

Yet that perfect June day, Luke looked out at the pastures of his youth and felt no affection for the graceful view before him. The grandeur of the prairie had lost its luster in his eye, and he knew he'd never be content to nestle down in Wyoming without leaving her familiar bosom first. If he didn't experience the firsthand reality of another world, a restless idleness would forever agitate his happiness. So when InterVarsity offered him and Paige an opportunity for adventure in Vancouver, they made their exodus from the Equality State, unsure if they'd ever return to stay.

During their time in Vancouver, Luke came to appreciate the spirit and beauty of the Pacific Northwest a great deal. The cherry blossoms in the spring. The autumn leaves bursting across the full spectrum of fall colors. The Pentecostal chatter of the produce markets—Indian, Eastern European, Chinese, Russian—echoing the ethnic and nutritional diversity of the region. It was a place of great bustling and life. One that prided itself on an open mind, tolerant heart and progressive attitude. In most aspects, Luke found these values to align in words and actions, with the exception of one specious case. In these liberal values, the Unchurched Belt—as it had been coined in the mid-eighties—thought itself to have very little in common with Christianity, therefore closing its mind to Christian ideas, not tolerating its beliefs, and repressing both its realistic outlook on the human heart and eternal optimism for the healing and restoration of it.

To say Christians in the Northwest were persecuted in the Roman sense of the word was hyperbolic. Nonbelievers in Vancouver didn't nail overzealous Bible thumpers to a cross upside-down. They didn't flog martyr-minded Jesus freaks in the public square. Hell, they'd see your crucifix necklace and still hold the door for you. No-no. The nature of these Pacific Coasters was too pacifistic for more tangible displays of maltreatment. They were not outright persecutors of the faith. They were, however, highly adept at being great, indifferent patronizers of it.

When Luke modestly unveiled his beliefs in conversation with the average secular Vancouverite, he could feel them reducing by half their regard for his intelligence. The same passive-aggressive condescending treatment the West Coast secularist would receive on vacation in the Bible Belt was tooth-for-tooth reciprocated to those copacetic with the Gospel on their own turf. On a dime, the mutual respect they'd shared before he claimed his Protestant allegiances turned into a one-sided evangelistic effort to awaken and turn him away from his ignoramus God-loving ways. Luke found what they despised most about Christianity wasn't actually Christ himself but the shortcomings of those trying to follow Him. Furthermore, the shortcomings of those they mistook for his closest followers. It seemed the first people that came to a secular Northwesterner's mind when they thought of Christians were the propagators of the Crusades, members of the KKK, and those who considered Rush Limbaugh their angry, political pastor. It was true these bastardized ideologies claimed to have been born under the roof of the Church, but the insinuation that Christ's example encouraged and blessed their conceptions—Luke thought that assumption was wholly inaccurate.

If he parried their argument with the likes of Martin Luther King Jr. and Nelson Mandela—more accurate examples of people who not only claimed but most closely imitated Christ's character, examples Northwesterners highly acclaimed as heroes of social justice, they merely dismissed them as great humanitarians. This seemed an odd quirk in the cognitive cultural development of the region. For all its cerebral scrupulousness, the Pacific Northwest never noticed the backward logic of beginning its examination of the Christian faith with the sheep—and even in that, starting with the blackest of the flock—instead of the shepherd.

No idea was more *out there* than believing it possible to turn fishermen into fishers of men. No heart so compassionate as the one who smiled warmly on lepers, tax collectors, and prostitutes. No statement so progressive in its time as turning the other cheek. Maybe the Pacific Northwest had little in common with Jerry Falwell, but in Jesus, they shared an incognizant kinship. So there Luke found himself—the leaves steadily, splendidly, shivering off the branches, the knitting of his firstborn near completion in Paige's womb, and an important decision to be made. The path of his and Paige's life had come to a fork in their journey. On the left was an urban life, seminary and the thrills and frustrations of guiding people in their relationships with God and each other. There were trees and water and public transportation, traffic, modish restaurants, light pollution and city parks. Since moving to Vancouver, he found, overall, its people—though a majority of them naive in their notions of the true Gospel—were like him, great respecters of free will and human dignity. It wasn't difficult to envision a fulfilling life spent trying to love these eccentric, reserved (and a bit sensitive) Northwestern souls.

On the right was the rural experience, finishing a ranching apprenticeship with his father to take over the Chugwater operation and the thrills and frustrations of making a living off the land. The perpetual gold-bathed prairie vistas contrasting gloriously with the floral combustions of dusk. The nearest grocery store twenty-five miles away. Stiff, monotonous winter winds blowing snow from the west into stubborn drifts—their forms conceived in December and still clinging crustily to the ground in February, daring the sun to warm enough to melt them. And above all, the splendor of the Wyoming night sky. So studded with stars you thought Heaven was on the brink of breaking through to dwell on Earth…

There Luke had found himself some nine years ago. The

same leather sphere he now held in the Steel Building he'd once held in an East Vancouver park—standing at the free-throw line as he was now, bouncing possibilities up and down as he was now, and it was there he'd discovered one of the great Christian truths many believers go their whole lives without being enlightened to—some paths are equal.

He'd spent months till then brooding over his decision. Searching like some novice diviner for "God's Will" in the matter, thinking one choice to be wicked defiance of that will and the other providentially blessed. Then, spinning the ball in his hands and snapping his wrist in textbook form—*swish!*—a great, progressive thought occurred to him—God could fit him into his divine plan whether he settled in Vancouver or Chugwater.

Maybe somewhere between destiny and decision, the Almighty authored his love story to creation.

Wasn't it possible that Luke's talents were equally suited for shepherding people *and* cattle? Didn't both souls and stomachs need to be fed? Weren't both—when approached with a thoughtful and humble heart—noble endeavors? Could not great lessons be learned in civilization and backcountry alike? The modern-day feud between city dwellers and rural settlers, thinking themselves intellectually or morally superior to their counterparts on account of their difference in habitat—it was stupid. It wasn't a matter of morality or intelligence at all, but one of preference. This was the consequence of fostering an over-individualistic culture—too many people mistook their personal preference for a moral compass.

Inching his right foot to the charity stripe, he tried to dial his focus on the back of the rim, but his usual Hoosieristic zen-like concentration was bemused by a sudden feeling of claustrophobia. Throughout his first six months in

Vancouver, Luke took nothing but pleasure in the formerly alien experience of living in a densely forested environment, but in an instant, his perception shifted to a swift disdain for them. Mutating from a cozy safe haven for his thoughts to the suffocating, unyielding barriers of his vision. And just as quickly, his former affections for that vast, still sea of prairie returned to him like the Prodigal Son.

How he longed to once again see out!

To drive without his foot touching the brake for half an hour. To be reunited with his favorite teacher (his father) in his favorite classroom (the pasture). Was there a simpler, more gratifying experience in the world than pulling a windmill with your father on a faultless Wyoming summer day?

He sank one last free throw and started walking the five blocks back to his and Paige's apartment above the house of the Sikh family they rented it from, where he found her on their rooftop deck tending her box garden.

"How are those carrots coming along?"

"Wonderfully!" Paige smiled. "Gardening's a little easier here than it is in Wyoming."

"And how's our girl?"

"Kicking like a kangaroo. She seems anxious to get out and see the world. Maybe when she graduates high school, I can take her to Peru. I'd love to go back." Luke nodded. "What's going on? You've got that look on your face you get when you have something on your mind." Paige inquired.

"Barring your consent, I was thinking about calling Dad and telling him he could expect us in Chugwater sometime in the spring."

"That's what you want?"

"Yes. I feel good about it."

"Then okay."

"And you? You're happy with going back?"

"Well," she grunted in the midst of severing a stout, bright orange carrot from the dirt, then held it up for Luke to see. "The bad news is you can't expect me to grow carrots of this quality in Chugwater. The good news is the one garden-variety plant that thrives in Wyoming is rhubarb, so I can make you all the rhubarb pie your heart desires."

"Life is a series of tradeoffs."

#

Back in the Steel Building, Luke was playing his old favorite game.

"Cowboys have the ball down one with twelve seconds on the clock. Anderson to inbound from the sideline. Moore comes off a pick and gets it at the top of the key. Passes it off to Bainbridge on the wing. Now follows his pass to set a screen on the ball. Seven seconds left! Bainbridge dribbles to the left. Splits the defense with a crossover! Pulls up! Shoots…"

Bank, swish!

"Yyyyyeesssss! Yessssss! Cowboys win! Cowboys win! In a rematch of the 1943 National Championship, Wyoming has once again shocked the Georgetown Hoyas to win the NCAA title! Oh! My! Goodness! What a game! The score! Ohhh the score! Cowboys ninety, Hoyas eighty-nine!"

He galloped around the Steel Building in wild, elated circles—hugging his imaginary teammates, jumping up and down. After a few laps, he stopped to catch his breath and come back to reality. The sadness was still there, but the small semblance of relief he didn't feel driving back from

Cheyenne had found him. Luke would miss his wife sleeping by his side. Nevertheless, the truth he'd spoken to her all those years ago in Vancouver still rang true.

Life was a series of tradeoffs.

Some of those trades were uneven, but sometimes all a person could do was take small comforts in the silver linings. Sleep would be hard to find in the nights ahead, but at least he could toss and turn without having to worry about rousing Paige's pain.

The day ahead of him loomed, especially if it snowed more than six inches and he had to feed hay so the range cake wouldn't disappear in the drifts. He didn't run the traditional cow-calf ranch most urbanites thought of when they were stuck at their desk job dreaming of becoming a cowboy. Luke got steers at around 500 pounds starting in November, beefed them up to about a thousand, then shipped them in September. A steer was the designated moniker of a male after they'd been castrated. Contrary to what most city folks said, most of the beef they'd eaten wasn't a cow, but a steer. Like people, a herd did best when they were fed seven days a week. During winter, the pasture grass was pale and fruitless. Cattle would forage it to stave off hunger, but it was a means of survival, not growth—like people in poverty eating Wonder Bread because it's cheap.

For the Hodge and Bainbridge Ranch to earn enough money to buy their families that nice grainy bread, they needed their cattle not just to survive the winter months but to thrive in them. To accomplish this, every morning from November to early April, Luke fed his herds a protein concentrate called range cake. Imagine a pellet of cat food only twenty times bigger and absent of the smell of feet dipped in gravy. The range cake substituted for all the green, nutritious, weight-gaining stuff the grass didn't provide until spring came (providing it was gracious enough to bring rain along with it). Each steer got two pounds of cake per day. That saying the mailman used about rain, sleet, snow or hail—he'd stolen it from a rancher. The rancher just couldn't prove it because his customers couldn't quote one-liners.

Compared to a rancher, a mailman was a part-time flower-delivery boy.

Because even when it was Saturday morning and a foot of last night's snow had been blown by thirty-mile-an-hour gusts into three-foot drifts, if Luke wanted his girls to eat that nice grainy bread, it was his duty to get his rear out of bed and break down the white-walled barriers separating him and his truck loaded with cake from three hundred starving cattle, all of whom were scattered about in any number of herds and waiting to be fed somewhere in a high-hilled, scrub-brushed pasture about the size of Central Park. Sure, Luke could take a day off. The cattle would suffer, but they wouldn't die. But that would make him a poor rancher, and Luke Bainbridge wasn't in that business. To skip tomorrow's feeding wouldn't be showing the very creatures that provided for his family the compassion and honor they deserved.

The cowboy had always been a symbol of nobility, and he couldn't call himself one if he cowered in his warm bed while three hundred other living things went hungry in the biting, wind-chilled cold. Every day he fed his cattle in the winter, they each gained about a half-pound. If he stayed in bed, that was a hundred and fifty pounds of beef he wouldn't have to sell come shipping time. This meant his family would only be able to afford Wonder Bread, which was something he couldn't afford to do. Maybe the crappy white stuff tasted better, but in the long term, the nice grainy bread nourished thicker skin. Denser, more fibrous bones. Thick skin and dense bones that could endure west-whipping winds when Luke had to fasten chains on his tires stuck in three feet of snow.

Back in the house, he entered his room and saw the empty bed, then forced himself under the covers without setting an alarm. Tomorrow was Saturday. No school. No church. No alarm. He would sleep until he woke. The cattle would have to wait a little longer than usual for breakfast, but he extended himself that small grace. Exhaustion was a sure way to make the daunting mountains of life loom larger than they already were.

#

Luke woke around nine to the smell of…was that…bacon?

If his nose was playing a trick on him, it was a damn dirty rotten one. *Please be true*, he thought. *Please be bacon. I don't think I can choke down one more fricking bowl of All-Bran.*

He got out of bed and put on his robe, then followed the savory aroma through the den to the kitchen. The girls were eating at the kitchen table as his mother milled about flipping strips of crispy bacon, cracking eggs, slathering jelly on toast.

"Hi, Mom."

"Good morning Luke!"

"Morning girls."

"Morning Dad."

"What's all this?"

"We thought maybe it'd be nice to come spend the day with you and the girls. I figured you haven't been eating a lot of hot breakfast these days. Hope it's okay I helped myself to the kitchen. Sorry we didn't call. Your dad and I wanted to surprise you."

"Don't apologize. This is wonderful, really. Dad here?"

"He left about an hour ago to feed for you. Would you like a plate?"

"Yes please. And he didn't have to do that. I could've gone out with him."

"He thought maybe you could use a morning off," she said, setting the heaping plate in front of him.

"That was kind of him. I have a gate in the Harry I need to brace this afternoon though."

"Maybe after lunch, the two of you can go out together and work on it…salt?"

"No, thank you. It really couldn't taste any better."

Marion smiled, then started in on the dishes.

#

The weatherman had fibbed.

Only four inches of snow had blanketed the prairie as Luke and Kirk went about bracing the wind-loosed gate in the Harry pasture. Years of cattle bruising into it on drives and persistent gusts heaping snowdrifts on its barbed shoulders had destabilized it.

Yet no such winds persisted as Luke and Kirk loosened the wires. It was a fine December afternoon in southeast Wyoming. Low-to-mid-forties. The air brisk and fresh. The still snow evincing the brilliance of a clear, sunny sky with a mystical glitter. All was calm and bright as father and son removed rotted gate posts and mangled staples, replacing them with successors, splicing and tautening wires, talking when they had something to say and working in agreeable silence when they didn't. They talked politics and the weather, the new family who had just moved into the old Miller place, the rumors of Denver getting its own professional baseball team. They discussed new theories in ranching, old cowboy proverbs that once again proved themselves true, potential future projects that could improve the ranch's staying power.

They didn't talk much about Paige. As they had the past forty months, Kirk asked about the current state of things, Luke stated the facts, and that was about the extent of it. The bond between them was deeply respectful, keenly understood and largely unspoken. In his own constrained way, Kirk had always shown a heartfelt adoration for Paige. Though never stated outright, Luke knew his father was beyond sorry for what had happened to her and how it had affected his son and granddaughters. There were times Luke wished they could find a natural way to delve a little deeper into the subject, but he never felt like his father wasn't there for him because he was, well, there. On a day when the isolation of ranching would've been a supremely lonely affair, his father had arrived to extend his help and steady company.

And it was okay they weren't really talking about Paige. That morning Luke didn't need a therapist to flounder with him in his floundering feelings. He just needed his father to be there, talking weather and politics and sports and ranching like they always had. They pounded the last few staples in the brace post, tested the unshakeable gate and took a step back to admire their good work.

"Oughtta steady her for a while at least," Kirk remarked.

"Yep. It's one of those jobs you can do by yourself, but is a heck of a lot easier with four hands instead of two. Thanks for coming down today. Things have been pretty tough around here lately. Really appreciate the help."

"Not a problem. Sometimes the old to-do list seems pretty endless, doesn't it?"

"Yes it does."

"I guess all you can do is just take it one day at a time. I've found if you can just focus on doing what you can each day, eventually things have a way of working out."

CHAPTER 18

A Sanctuary, a Cemetery and a Bar

May 20, 1991—Cheyenne, WY ||

It had been years since Aaron had found himself in a church.

Not like he'd ever really *found* himself in a church, but he couldn't remember the last time he'd physically been in one. They'd always made him uncomfortable, accompanied by a stout feeling of not belonging. Never much for small talk, it seemed to Aaron every congregation in every sanctuary he'd ever been in was particularly fond of surface-level gab. And even though it had probably been a decade since he was last inside one, the aura of awkwardness greeted him immediately upon wheeling through the doors of Calgary Baptist. Stiff wooden pews and drawling electric organs. Watery coffee and powdered creamer. The smells of old paper, old carpet and old lady's perfume.

He was there though. For Chuck. For Dye. All he had to do was endure the next ninety minutes. Ignore the Baptist dogma. Avoid conversations with overbearing strangers trying to make him feel welcome. Bite his tongue when he wanted to make a wisecrack to his sister about religion.

Ninety minutes.

If he could do that, he would fulfill his duties as the brother of his recently widowed sister, honoring Chuck in her way. Then he could head downtown to The Albany and honor his brother-in-law in Aaron's way—drinking a few pints and reminiscing about Chuck with his cousins who'd flown in from New England.

"I was thinking after this is over we could get a group together for some beers downtown." He told his favorite cousin, Barry, as they waited in the foyer for the service to start.

"Sounds like a plan to me," Barry said, then pointed his eyes at a woman and her son who had just entered the sanctuary. "You gonna invite her?"

Alicia Zielinski might as well have come in through the ceiling, so divine did she appear to Aaron. Her golden-brown hair, which had always run to the middle of her back, had been tapered just past her shoulders to match her age. She wore a black trench coat with the belt tied very sexily around her waist. Her lipstick a few shades darker than the last time he saw her over a decade ago, causing her blue-green eyes to burst evermore.

Clinging to her right hand was her son, Lionel, looking almost nothing like his father and everything like her. He had her fine hair and galactic, grinning eyes, though the combination of Alicia and Gary had produced a nose that looked eerily like Aaron's, who couldn't decipher if his head was swimming, spinning, soaring or all three at once. Somehow, they all seemed appropriate to describe the cosmic inter-weavings of past, present and future, churning out a tapestry of destiny and decision before him.

What was she doing here? he wondered, his thoughts catching up with the situation. But of course, she was there.

She always loved Chuck and Dye, and Denver was only a hundred miles south of Cheyenne. Was it possible she also thought she'd have a chance to see Aaron? How did she hear about it though? Someone must've called her. Whoever they were, he wanted to find them and kiss their sweet, thoughtful brow …

Suddenly, Aaron found himself thrilled to be in church as he approached Alicia and her son talking to Dye. "Hey Leash."

She turned and smiled like stars exploding. "Hi! I've never seen you in a tie before. It's…you look nice."

"Thanks. You look great. I like your hair like that."

"Thank you," she said and looked down at Lionel. "Sweetie, this is Diana's brother, Aaron. He's funny. I think you'd like him if you gave him a chance. Can you say hi please?"

Reluctantly, Lionel looked up at Aaron.

"Hey dude," Aaron said nonchalantly, then offered a sturdy and peculiarly shaped hand to which Lionel shook after a moment of internal debate.

"You don't look like brother and sister," Lionel said, looking at Aaron, then Diana.

"We were adopted."

"What's adopted?"

"It's when people have a baby, but for whatever reason they can't take care of them, so they give them to people who can't have babies but want some to take care of."

Lionel processed that for a moment, then said with a pensive, childlike matter-of-factness, "My dad doesn't take care of me very much."

"Lucky for you, you have a great mom who I'm sure takes very good care of you."

"How do you know my mom?"

Aaron and Alicia exchanged a quick glance. "Back when I was in school, before I needed this wheelchair, I was friends with your Uncle Ty."

"And then you became friends with my mom?"

"Pretty much."

"Why do you need a wheelchair?"

"I was swimming and fell in the water and hurt my neck. Turns out if you hurt your neck bad enough, you can't walk anymore. Lucky for me, your Uncle Ty was there, so I didn't drown when I got hurt."

"Ouch."

"Yep. *Ouch.*"

"That stinks. So you can't go swimming anymore?"

"Nope. I go kayaking though. Do you know what that is?"

Lionel shook his head.

"It's like a little boat for one person."

"Maybe sometime I can go swimming, and you can bring your kayak?"

"I'd like that dude."

The sound of the organ dribbled out into the foyer, signaling the service was about to begin. "I better get in there," Diana said. "Great to see you Alicia. Are you going back to Denver after the service?"

"We haven't decided. Might just get a hotel and head back in the morning."

"Well, if you end up staying, some of my friends have offered to watch the boys tonight after the service. I'm sure they wouldn't mind looking after Lionel too. Give you and Aaron a chance to talk more."

"I might take you up on that."

"Do. Alright, I better go. See you in there." Diana leaned

down to hug her brother.

"Thanks," he whispered in her ear.

"For what?" She winked.

#

The service was strangely wonderful.

Aaron did things he'd never done in a church before—he cried, he laughed, he sang. Yes, he sang. Some unbeknownst flame bore itself in his chest, igniting his tongue as he belted out "Amazing Grace." He sang like he did "Angie" with Ty as they drove to the swimming hole on the first day of school. It was good to sing, to laugh and cry. It was good to be with the people in that sanctuary. Even if he didn't know most of them, it didn't matter. They all knew and loved Chuck. They could all agree on that one thing, and Aaron wouldn't call it asking Jesus into his heart, but he realized something like an epiphany during his brother-in-law's funeral. Maybe there was something to the Gospel of Christ. Maybe we were all impossibly, irreconcilably different, but if we could ever agree on just one thing—that each of us was flawed, incapable of being our own or anyone else's savior, that if we could resign ourselves to becoming our true, redeemed selves, being there for each other when that resolve began to falter—if we all came to that conclusion, maybe the world would stop tearing itself apart and start mending itself back together.

For the first time, Aaron found himself in a church and the spirit of the place actually emanated what it always claimed to be—an oasis in a spiritual desert for the weary and heavy-laden to rest, where the earnest-hearted and outcasted found belonging, where the widow could freely weep and the orphans were fathered by a heavenly love.

#

The gravesite was a few miles north of town on a gentle, grassy slope looking north toward Chugwater (land of the "world famous" chili). His final resting place had a modest but elegant view of the long-rolling, sage-speckled prairie that had beckoned Chuck to Wyoming. Behind the plot, three young pines grappled to take root against the wind in their infancy, looking as though, in time, they'd grow high and strong. Billowing May clouds hovered like frozen explosions on the western horizon, the sun glinting off the massive plumes, tinging their ivory with gold. The weather was suspended in a state of indecision—a little warm for a jacket, the persistent breeze making it chilly without one.

"Are we going to grab a drink after this is over or what?" Alicia whispered, appearing suddenly next to Aaron, snapping him out of the staring contest he'd been having with a yellow-breasted meadowlark resting on one of the pines as the pallbearers prepared to lower Chuck's body in place.

"You're staying?"

"Yes. Preferably at your hotel if they have a room available—that way, we can split a cab back from the bar."

"Cab?"

"Unless you're planning to be sober enough to drive. I won't be though. Single moms have to take advantage of a night out on the town."

"Let me tell you—you've never lived until you've gone out in downtown Cheyenne on a Tuesday night."

Somebody played "It Is Well" on a violin as they began lowering the casket. A slight surge rose in the breeze. The meadowlark on the branch of the pine flew away, a slight *thud* reverberating amidst the mourners as the casket settled in its resting place.

#

In its own way, The Albany had a certain romantic charm to it.

A red-bricked building, three stories—sky-scraping by Wyoming standards. Twin double-hung windows framed in pine-green trim. Inside, cherry-brown leather and brass-buttoned booths. Wide-planked wood floors. The lighting not too dim or bright. Rich, arching woodwork backed the bar, encasing mirrors reflecting amber and crystal glows from the bottles of liquor.

Aaron, Alicia and Barry all split a cab there from the hotel. The driver was generous to halt the meter while Aaron transferred out, which took longer than usual as he figured out the specifics of transferring out of that specific vehicle. Others from the service trickled in. To Aaron's surprise, one of them was his sister, who he'd invited half in jest. She declined his offer for a shot of whiskey but seemed content to be in the company of those closest to Chuck as she sipped her glass of merlot. Eventually, Aaron and Alicia drifted to their own booth in the corner, Aaron parking at the end of the table.

"I've wanted to call you so many times over the years, I just—" Aaron confessed, their recently downed second shot of bourbon tingling in his cheeks.

"Didn't know where to start…"

"Yes. I was an idiot to drive you away. I told myself I was doing what was best for you, but I dunno, I guess—I dunno…I figured down the road you'd realize you didn't want me and leave."

"What did I ever do to make you think I was that kind of person?"

"You left for college."

"You didn't try very hard to make me stay."

"I wanted you to want to stay."

"I would've stayed—I just wanted you to want me to." They laughed.

"You know I'm not good at asking for things."

"Well, let's work on that. Ask me for something."

Aaron held up his beer, nearly empty, implying he wanted another.

"No! You dick," she laughed, slapping his shoulder. "I'm talking something significant. Something that makes you feel vulnerable."

"Like?"

"Like ask me for another chance."

"What do you mean? You want me to move to Denver? You want to move back to Milwaukee?"

"For God's sake, Aaron, one step at a time."

"Alright. Fine. Will you give me another chance?"

She hooked a hand around the back of his neck, her crimson fingernails touching the scar running down the middle. Then she pulled her chest to his, kissing him like men dream of being kissed—with passion, with urgency and confidence. He kissed back, tugging slightly at her bottom lip with his teeth before she pulled away and said, "Sure, I'll give you another shot. Let's not fuck it up this time."

CHAPTER 19

When Your Miller Needs a Bud

September 13, 1991—Milwaukee, WI ||

Hank downed his last swig of Miller Lite and considered becoming an alcoholic.

He liked his brandy Manhattan before dinner and a glass of red with it, had always enjoyed the little jolt of electricity it gave to life, but he'd never felt an unquenchable thirst for the potential numbness alcohol offered until he looked over with trepidation at his grandsons intently watching Robin Yount take batting practice from their seats right behind the dugout and the empty bottle of beer in his hand carried a weight beyond the absence of liquid.

Grief's most winning quality had always been its indelibility. It had a bad habit of making the most simply joyful moments all the more miserable. Here Hank was, drinking a beer at County Stadium on a pleasant Milwaukee late-summer afternoon with Jeremy and Mick. A Hallmark moment, if ever there was one. The boys seemed to be finding escape in America's past-time. Maybe watching Yount, Chuck's favorite baseball player, made it feel, in a way, like he was alive again for a few hours. Still, all Hank could think was—*my son is dead*. And—*how will I ever look at my grandsons without being reminded of that?*

"You want another beer Hank?" Warren asked.

Warren was Hank's friend, the newly appointed president and CEO of Miller Brewing Company and a good man. Hank and his grandsons had Warren's generosity to thank for their VIP seats. He had also funded the two cold ones Hank had polished off in the last forty-five minutes.

"Yes—" Hank replied, swallowing a lump in his throat. "Please."

"Coming right up," Warren said with a sympathetic wink, then held up a finger to the vendor. Hank was somewhat embarrassed to be out-boozing the executive of a major American beer company, but if he stopped drinking, he'd start crying. An act he was determined not to make his grandsons witness that day. Before Chuck died, the thought of damming his tears never crossed his mind. For as long as Hank could remember, whenever he felt like crying, he let them pour out without hesitation. It was a quality that never made him question his manhood until he watched his son's brilliance be erased before his eyes in a matter of eleven months, then die.

"Here ya go Hank…Hank?"

"Yeah?"

"Here's your beer."

"Oh, yeah. Thanks Warren."

"You alright?"

"Fine thanks," he said, taking a large swill from the bottle. "Just got caught up in enjoying the view." He leaned forward and squinted his eyes, pretending to focus in on Yount's swift, sage swing as John Prine's "Bruised Orange (Chain of Sorrow)" came on through the PA speakers. He watched Yount batter four straight balls to the opposite field, but Hank wasn't remotely thinking about baseball. He was thinking about Chuck and John Prine and the Paradise Steam Plant in Muhlenberg County, Kentucky.

His twangy voice and titillating lyrics had been the catapult for the whole catastrophe that were Hank and Chuck's political "conversations." Before Chuck ever listened to "Paradise," he and Hank had begun to have small, relatively civil partisan disagreements throughout his son's senior year of high school. Then somewhere between starting his freshman year at Dartmouth and Christmas break, someone introduced Chuck to the folky songwriter's self-titled debut album, which he practically came to consider the fifth Gospel of Jesus Christ.

As they sat down to Christmas dinner, Chuck looked across the table and asked his father if he was familiar with a piece of mining equipment nicknamed Big Hog. Of course, Hank was. Over the trajectory of his career, he'd worked his way up to the title of Head of International Sales for Bucyrus-Erie, the very company that'd sold Big Hog to Peabody Energy for their operation at the Sinclair Strip Mine, which shipped a nonstop supply of coal to power the Paradise Steam Plant. As it was located in the States, Hank himself hadn't been involved in the deal, but everyone at Bucyrus—hell, everyone who worked in the mining industry—was familiar with Big Hog. It was, in its prime, the mining engineering marvel of its age. The biggest, most brutish shovel the world had ever seen. So big Bucyrus-Erie had to build it on-site piece by piece. Even then, the individual parts were so large a special spur rail had to be laid to ship them in. Once assembled, it stood about twenty stories high, weighed around nine thousand tons, and was capable of devouring a hundred and seventeen tons of earth in a single bite.

It was the strip miner's dream.

Then Chuck asked his father if he was aware that Big Hog was the engine responsible for the annihilation of many of Kentucky's proudest mountains, the pollution and devastation of their most beautiful river, as well as the virtual murder of the small, peaceful town of Paradise. It wasn't like Hank had never wrestled with the ethical dilemmas of working in the mining industry. It was true that little towns like Paradise were the peaceful, unfortunate souls in the way of the greater good, and that didn't make him smile, but the coal the strip mines provided beamed electricity to millions of homes in America.

Was a warm house a bad thing?

Hank had to admit he might feel differently if he'd grown up in Muhlenberg County. And yes, Bucyrus had been the foe of some of the world's natural beauty, but it wasn't like Hank hated nature. Chuck's generation always acted like they owned the block on environmentalism, but it was Hank's and the one before his who'd designated the National Parks. There were still plenty of places to enjoy creation. Idealism wanted a forest in their backyard and a fully stocked grocery store in the front. Reality didn't permit that. Comprises had to be made. The world was both growing and wanting to grow more comfortable. Humanity was tired of pumping its own water. Tired of it taking hours for our food to be ready to eat. Tired of breaking horses and traveling at three miles per hour.

Hank landed the job at Bucyrus-Erie shortly out of college, and he couldn't have been more grateful for the clutch timing of the opportunity. Right after graduating with an engineering degree from William & Mary, he married Rosie a week later and got her pregnant shortly after, leaving him with cold reality staring him in the face. He needed a good job to provide for his family. Bucyrus-Erie had offered him that as an export sales correspondent, and he'd made notable sacrifices to capitalize on it. Shortly after Chuck was born, they asked Hank to go to Brazil for six months to try and sell equipment to a big mining operation there. Six months with no way to communicate with his family but snail mail. Six sexless months—living, eating, and sleeping in a hotel in a country whose language he didn't speak. Six awfully lonely months. But it was his chance to move up the ladder, so he went, and when he got back and bent down on his knee to hug his two-year-old son for the first time in six months—Chuck, not recognizing him, backed away suspiciously, turned to his mother and said, "I want my real dad. *He's* in Brazil."

Did Chuck realize how that had nearly killed him? That Hank had once been held at gunpoint in Zaire, almost died in a plane crash in the Congo, had—to fulfill his obligations as the guest of honor and seal the deal—eaten duck brain in China, drank turtle blood in Mongolia? That he'd missed precious time with his family traveling months out of the year to Australia, Japan, Scandinavia, Jamaica and Chile? Over the next few years, more heated disagreements of this nature ineluctably surfaced at the Westerman dinner table. Until finally, Rosie banished any talk of politics while they ate, or for that matter, when she was in the room.

In many ways, Chuck was the son of Hank Westerman. He'd gotten his sharp, analytical mind, his self-confidence with a tendency to turn into arrogance. His playful, affectionate heart. But where the conservative philosophy came naturally to Hank, his son seemed to have inherited more liberal convictions. While it was a difference that played out with hostility in their talks of politics, in other areas of their relationship, Hank had found their polarities as fascinating as their similarities.

Though he and Rosie had taken their kids to church growing up, they were never pietistic in their approach to religion. They weren't always harping on the Gospel or desperately trying to bully their neighbors into believing in Christ and Hell as absolute truths. They thought it was a good way to instill some moral fiber in their kids. After John, their youngest, left the house, Hank and Rosie essentially scaled back their attendance to just Christmas and Easter. John and Katie were tepid about their churchgoings growing up, but Chuck took his little cracker and shot of grape juice with full devotion to the idea. He got genuinely giddy for youth group and church camps, volunteered on his own accord at a municipal pool helping kids with disabilities learn how to swim, and had read through the entire Bible at least twice by the time he graduated high school.

He wasn't self-righteous when it came to his faith though. Now his intelligence, *that* he could be obnoxiously pompous about. Boggle, Trivial Pursuit, Risk—Chuck wasn't shy about letting his opponents know they were inferior to him when it came to these pastimes. But his faith didn't turn his heart to fire and brimstone. He really did care about the widows and the poor, really respected them as people and tried to help give them opportunities to prosper. Rosie used to go into Milwaukee and volunteer with a Head Start program that tutored five-year-olds in the inner-city, trying to prepare them for first grade, so maybe that's where Chuck got some of it from. Wherever exactly it *had* come from, Hank didn't know, but he was always proud of the profession his son had chosen. And he liked to think that—though maybe

Chuck didn't agree with Hank's political views—his father had played a significant role in modeling how to love the people close to him…

Yount finished batting practice with one last blast to the opposite field as Prine strummed the last chord of "Bruised Orange." Paul Molitor stepped next into the box in place of Yount. Sinatra sang "It's Up to You New York" in place of Prine.

Ah, Sinatra.

Now *there* was something Hank and Chuck never had a problem agreeing on. Old Blue Eyes had been playing in the background as father and son had their final conversation in CRMC…

He couldn't fight it any longer.

Despite his promise to himself, a tear careened from Hank's eyes. Surrendering, he put his head down, brought a hand to his brow and permitted his body to tremble. Warren plucked him from the seas of memory as he put a gentle hand on Hank's back and held up his bottle of beer. "To Chuck."

Hank looked up at his friend with a sad smile and echoed the toast, then drained the last of his Miller. "Thanks Warren. For everything."

"Least I could do. You want another beer?"

"You know, I think I'm alright."

"How 'bout a story then?"

"A story?"

"Yeah. A good Chuck story. One from before he got sick."

Hank thought for a while, and England came to mind. The whole family had lived in Lincoln for two years as part of another step up the Bucyrus-Erie ladder. Chuck, nine at the time, loved the experience. Said he felt like he fit in more naturally in Britain than his native country. "We sent Chuck to this all-boys school, and one day his teacher was giving a lecture on British history. He kept asking questions none of the boys knew the answers to, except Chuck, of course. Finally, after this happened about four or five times, the teacher threw his chalk down in disgust and yelled, 'Are you all just gonna sit here and let this damn Yankee disgrace you in your knowledge of your own country?'

"The funny thing was though, he was still a big hit with all the boys in his class. There weren't many circles he couldn't fit into. So the week before we're about to move back to Milwaukee, on Chuck's last day of school, Rosie goes to pick him up. She steps out of the car, and there's Chuck! Riding on the shoulders of his classmates, and they're singing 'He's a Jolly Good Fellow.'"

Warren smiled at the end of Hank's story, then turned his head to the man who had appeared before them in the aisle next to their seat. He had a stern, slack face with shifty eyes. A constant, drooping frown and large, round-cornered glasses. His hair was toast-colored, very thin, and Hank wasn't sure if he liked him. The man smiled and shook hands with Warren. "Hank, this is Mr. Selig—the owner of the Milwaukee Brewers."

"I'm familiar with the name," Hank said, reaching out and accepting Bud Selig's handshake. "Thank you for the seats."

"Not a problem Mr. Westerman." His face broke out in a good-natured smile, causing Hank to reverse his first impression. "Warren told me about the tragedy that has befallen your family, and I just want to say you have my and the entire Brewers organization's condolences. If you'd like, we have some gifts to give your grandsons, and if they're interested, we've made arrangements for a tour of the clubhouse."

Hank looked over at Jeremy and Mick, their eyes as big as baseballs, looking at Bud Selig like they did when they saw Santa Claus in the Cheyenne Frontier Mall. "I think they'd be interested in that…right boys?"

"Absolutely!" Jeremy shouted as Mick nodded his wooden head so emphatically Hank thought it might fall off.

#

Yount was leaning over the fence, watching Molitor as they were led into the dugout.

Thud!

"Good cut, Paul," he said, then looked over to see Hank and his grandsons approaching, Jeremy wearing the shirt Chuck gave him—a screen print of a cartoon Robin Yount following through on his swing, his head bobble-sized in proportion to the rest of his body with flames licking out from the back of his mullet. "Nice shirt kid!"

"Thanks Mr. Yount! Um, would you mind giving us your autograph?"

"That depends. Do you have a pen?"

"I've got a marker!"

"That'll do. What's your name?" he said as he signed Jeremy's program.

"Jeremy."

"Nice to meet you Jeremy."

"And I'm Mick. Like Mick Jagger. Could you sign mine too?"

"Sure Mick Jagger."

"You were my dad's favorite baseball player."

"I was?"

"Yeah."

"Sounds like your dad was a very smart man."

"Yep."

CHAPTER 20

The No Dwelling Place

March 6, 1992–Cheyenne, WY ||

Diana couldn't sleep.

It was three in the morning, and all she wanted to do was vacuum the living room. When Chuck died, she went from vacuuming frequently to vacuuming incessantly. She had no say in the death of her husband, but whether or not the carpet was clean—that she could do something about. But she couldn't vacuum because it was three in the morning and she'd wake the boys. She had to do something though, because sleep wasn't coming. Every time her eyes closed, she saw all her bad thoughts again.

A pea. It was just this little pea-sized thing. But it was so much bigger than that. It was an asteroid. An otherworldly cosmic stone in his head which collided with her galactic wooden heart. Her heart had been consumed by a black hole. This was her universe. A flaming asteroid swallowed by a black hole. The universe was all just one big cosmic astronomical mind-fuck. And he was never coming back. The father of her children—Never. Ever. Coming. Back. And it was all just because of this stupid little pea-sized problem that became an asteroid getting swallowed in a black hol—

"No!" she said aloud in her bed. "You're not going to do this Dye. You said you weren't going to dwell, so stop dwelling."

She wouldn't dwell. She would cope.

Coping was alcohol poured in a deep cut. Burned like hell, healed like Jesus. Dwelling was gasoline. It got in the wound and infected her hope. And if she dwelled long enough, the infection would get so bad she'd break out in a spiritual fever and get delusional—start thinking life was nothing but a deep cut with gasoline in it or a flaming asteroid in a black hole.

#

This wasn't Diana's first encounter with family tragedy.

A thought that struck her—albeit in a twisted way—as good news. Giving her a kind of preconceived confidence in her belief that some semblance of light at the end of the tunnel wasn't merely a false perception of hope but a possible reality to obtain, barring she kept nudging her thoughts in its direction. It was a funny quirk of hers—in the smaller contritions of life, she could be quite the harper. The gift of having a large, open heart came with an effortless ability to achieve sincere intimacy over a cup of coffee with anyone willing to open their own. The curse was it was always open season on her emotions. Whenever she sang at church, which was often, she could still hear her father's single, callous observation that her performance of "Battle Hymn of the Republic" when she was eighteen "sounded a little flat."

A week after moving into her dorm at the University of Wisconsin Eau-Claire, she got the terrible call from her parents that her brother had been in a diving accident and couldn't wiggle his toes. She was surprised to find the spiritual gifts of exhortation and perseverance came quite naturally to her in the midst of the Hamilton family crisis. From an early age, she'd recognized a very clear and important distinction between dwelling on and coping with the major hardships of life.

Spending little time wasting over *what if?* or *how could this happen?* or *if only we would have?* At eighteen, Diana took her place in the family as the spiritual rock. After all, Aaron *was* alive. Dexterity of the limited variety was better than no dexterity at all. The parts of his body that still worked were young, strong and capable of bearing the yoke upon him. And what better person was there to conquer the stubborn task ahead than her defiant little brother? His larger-than-life persona was tailor-made for what had, in a single swing, become his defining purpose in life—to live autonomously.

A purpose Diana thought an utterly humble but infinitely meaningful reason to get out of bed in the morning. For Aaron's purpose was, on a more exaggerated scale, the purpose of all humanity—to live with dignity as a free man within the confines of an imprisoned and indignant existence. It was out of this revelation she eventually found her own professional passion and purpose. Of all the ways she could go about helping the world, none came more naturally than valuing the least of these.

The strange thing about Diana Westerman was that she liked people.

Like *really* liked them. Lived for them. Valued them. Tortured herself when she felt she'd let them down. If she missed a note singing in church, burned her lasagna when she had company or ran out of time to vacuum the stairs before hosting company—these personal blunders were examined with the thorough, invasive nature of a colonoscopy.

Music, food, hospitality—Diana had converted the left side of her chest into a big, comfy room large enough to host their myriad of company. She enjoyed these things because they were all rivers eventually spilling into the ocean of her ultimate joy that was bringing people together.

There was no doubt in her mind becoming a Christian had changed the way she loved people for the better, but whether or not she'd ever uttered the sinner's prayer, she felt she would've liked them just the same. Pearly gates and streets of gold seemed alright to Diana, but her ideal of Heaven was a big, inviting dinner table. A tasteful, healthy feast before it, and the whole spectrum of humanity gathered around—dressed to the nines in their true colors.

Like she liked people, Diana liked colors.

She could never figure out if she liked people because she liked colors or if she liked colors because she liked people…sort of the philosophical "chicken or the egg" of her existence. Either way, they seemed to be intertwined—colors and people. United as they were in her cognitive amalgamation, like the brain itself, one clear distinction separated the left (colors) from the right (people), and it was the Gospel that first helped her make it. A distinction that could best be explained by performing a kind of literary lobotomy on Diana's brain.

Her left brain had concluded that colors were certain of their true character.

She'd always been awestruck at the flawlessness with which God had placed each and every color in the world. If the sky were turquoise instead of blue, maybe this wouldn't have been the case. A turquoise sky would be overbearing—too much volume for a loud color. No. The soft, subtle energy of sky blue coupled with the ivory tint of clouds perfectly. But a robust, quarter-sized turquoise stone naja hanging from a Navajo silver squash blossom necklace?

Its beauty struck her with the same reverence as the bluest of skies.

Everywhere she looked in the divine architecture of creation seemed to confirm the supernatural genius of the Creator. Not once had she thought the grass should not be green, the dirt not brown, the sun not gold. They all came together in perfect visual harmony. Each color had a distinct identity within the communal tribe of the spectrum. Before Chuck's funeral in May, black was the one color Diana didn't care for. Surprisingly, the daunting amount of it present at the service had been comforting. The tones of spring contained some of her most-liked colors—honeydew, lavender, peach, cherry red. They all lustered in her hazel eyes with the awakening of spring. Usually, she preferred those colors to the ominous pigment of black. In the ebony dead of winter, she longed for their sentient hues. But had her husband's mourners come to the funeral in the bright May colors aforementioned, her tears would've filled the baptismal pool instead of the lap of her dress because it would've been like the pot calling the kettle cherry red. No matter how beautiful the color, when it wasn't being used for its purpose in the world, when it was being worn dishonestly—pretending as if a thirty-four-year-old's funeral was a birthday party for a one-year-old—it simply didn't match and became revolting to her.

The right side of Diana's brain had concluded that people who were uncertain of their true colors didn't know their place in the world and, therefore, didn't feel a desire to contribute to it. One of the truths that had always kept Diana connected with her faith was the way Christianity revolutionized the way she found purpose in life. Jesus personally valued the individual, the uniqueness of each color. He wanted people to identify the distinct gifts they'd been given, which languages of love they spoke most fluently. He strived to encourage a world where everyone in it prospered, but he didn't endorse the kind of self-absorbed individualism that had taken hold of America over the last few decades. Jesus treasured the individual, yes, but they didn't take precedence over the community as a whole. A community functions at its best when all colors are present and in their right places. It was true that some people were sky blue and, hence, played a bigger role in the world than those who were turquoise, but the beauty was that the more prominent colors were no more important than their less renowned brothers and sisters.

The day she got the call about Aaron's accident would always be a day Diana looked back on with a degree of sadness, but she still found consolation in the fact that her first great personal tragedy led to her vocational purpose of persuading the world that turquoise was just as important as sky blue. A purpose she carried out in her work with the disadvantaged youth of Cabrini Green and the Rehabilitation Institute of Chicago, then later in Cheyenne, working in vocational rehab with a nonprofit that raised awareness for employers to hire and properly train people with disabilities. It boiled Diana's blood hot red when people only looked at Aaron in his wheelchair with pity, like he had nothing left to contribute to the world. It seemed perfectly clear to Diana we were all crippled in some sense of the word. In

Aaron's case, it was literal. Making him—in a very tangible way—invaluable for helping able-bodied understand their own disabilities, giving them hope they had the ability to overcome them, all the while reminding them to be thankful they didn't have to understand and overcome them so literally as her brother.

#

Charlie had been there when his mother made the decision not to dwell, sort of.

It was the night after they'd found out Chuck was terminal. Just moments after Diana finally fell into an emotionally exhausted slumber around three in the morning, Charlie started wailing. Weary, downtrodden, Diana got out of bed and swayed her youngest back and forth, back and forth, in a Denver hotel room. She looked out the window at the Mile-High lights, then into his tear-filled sage-green eyes, then back at the lights, then back into his eyes. As a tired, solitary tear trickled down his cheek, instead of seeing it as a tear of despair, she decided to interpret it as a drop of desperate hope. A tiny translucent crystal of living water pleading for his mother to stick to her true colors and lead them through the valley of the shadow.

"Lord," she prayed, "I can either be angry with You the rest of my life because You're in control and I'm not. Or I can accept that Your ways are not my ways, be faithful, and trust that somehow, you'll redeem all this."

So no. Diana had made her decision. She'd committed herself to not dwelling. She wouldn't think about the asteroid colliding with the black hole. She would cope. Whatever she had to do to cope. She'd vacuum till the Dirt Devil ate the fucking carpet. But as she lay in bed, anxious and wide awake, she couldn't vacuum because the boys were asleep, so she prayed. Tired prayers she'd prayed a thousand times over the last year. Prayers she wondered if God was tired of hearing.

Give me strength. Don't make it hurt so much. Don't let the boys grow up angry. Help me pay the bills. Help me. I feel so alone. Help me. I feel so alone. PLEASE. *Help me. I—*

I could bake, she thought.

She needed a dessert to bring to the grief support group the following afternoon. She didn't really want to go but knew not going would be dwelling and going would be coping, so she'd go.

Yes. Couldn't sleep. Couldn't vacuum. But she could bake. And she could take what she baked to the grief support group. And so, Diana Westerman got out of bed and made the best damn cream puffs the folks at the grief support group would ever have in their lives.

CHAPTER 21

Seventy Cattle x Seven Miles

March 6, 1992—Chugwater, WY, The Harry Pasture

Luke was tired.

Already he was sure it was the longest day he'd ever lived by noon. He'd awoken to a ripping wind making a real mess of the previous night's thirteen inches of snow. Haley slept in and missed the bus. Emma caught the bus but forgot her book report.

The three of them were doing the best they could. He ended up hiring Dana full-time, with part of her salary being room and board in the downstairs bedroom. She'd been worth every penny. Cooking, cleaning, providing the girls with some semblance of a matronly figure. But she'd gone back to Nebraska for the week to see family, leaving Luke on his own to take care of things around the house *and* the ranch.

Since Paige's death, Haley had been better about being ready for the bus. That morning though, she'd procrastinated getting out of bed as long as possible, then tried to feign a fever. He dropped her off by the playground to join her friends for morning recess. Mrs. Hazel was standing by the curb. When Luke asked if there was any reason Haley would want to skip school, Mrs. Hazel informed him Kyle Slater had been giving her a hard time again. The combination of fatherly instinct and Luke's hatred of those who inflict cruelty on the suffering had him near boiling at the thought of Kyle Slater's face when he got the call five minutes after getting home that Emma had forgotten her book report. There it was—laying on the breakfast table, colorful and organized, an A-plus report on *Amelia Bedelia Goes Camping*.

After making two unplanned trips to the school, he still had three hundred cattle to feed. He'd fed about seventy head before he got his truck stuck trying to take a shortcut down a sharp, narrow hill seven miles from the house. And not just stuck. *Stu-uck*—beyond the help of chains stuck. Don't even try digging out stuck. Walk seven miles through a foot of snow back to the house and get the tractor...stuck.

Post-holing the seven miles through hollowed drifts every fifth step or so, he tried not to think about Paige, but whenever he walked too long in the cold, his ankle started aching, and the memories throbbed...

His senior year of high school, he and Paige went ice skating during Christmas Break at Luther's Pond with her older brother Chris and the rest of the gang. Luke and Paige were holding hands and circling the pond lackadaisically when Chris raced up behind them and stole one of his sister's mittens. Luke chased after him, and though the best player on the Albin High basketball team, the same could not be said for his prowess on ice skates. As he bore down on his future brother-in-law, Chris—burly as a bull but surprisingly elegant on ice—made a sharp and graceful turn. Luke tried to stay with him, and the town of Albin's hopes of a state championship broke with his ankle when he went down awkwardly. He always regretted stepping on the ice that day. Why he didn't stop to consider everything he was risking was unlike him. But he had never regretted chasing after Chris once he was on the ice. If there was one thing he hated more than anything, it was the thought of a woman's hands being cold.

He didn't know which he was angrier at—the cancer or the morphine. It wasn't the cancer that killed her. Cancer in your bones didn't shut your organs down. It just sat there, sucking all but the last breath out of the most beautifully alive woman he'd ever known.

Cancer—what a clown. It didn't even have the decency to kill her. Just sat there. Three years it sat there until finally, the excess of morphine she needed to kill the pain shut her organs down.

He tried to take his mind off his ankle by counting all the different colors he could see hidden on the prairie, but the snow hid the subtle nuances. Even the one all-encompassing cloud above his head looked like a big quilt of gray snow. The sun snuggled under it, too warm and cozy to come out. He tried to think about snow, but he could only dwell on how it was cold and beautiful. Like Paige's hand when Chris stole her glove and Luke went chasing after him and broke his ankle. He continued his plod through the snow to the tractor, his thoughts spinning stagnantly in drifts of fear and anger.

Her hands were cold. I'd break my ankle for that every time. Pain. Morphine. Pain. Morphine. I'd still chase after him. Hands. Snow. Cold. Beautiful. They'll never be warm again. You can't put mittens on a dead person in the ground. She was so beautiful. Died so coldly. Pain. Morphine. Pain. Morphine.

"God dammmiit!" he thundered out of the silence. "It's always so fucking quiet out here! All there is to do is think! Say something dammit! Why'd ya have to do it like that huh? C'mon! Just say something! Anything! All you did was sit up there and say nothing! You just sat there!"

Luke dropped to his knees, inanimate and out of breath, his eyes staring down at the snow around him as he waited for an audible reply to his lament, but all he could hear was the same old murmuring hymn of the January wind and he was utterly sick of it. He'd grown up with this song. Had heard its strains a thousand times before. Still, in his stolid desperation, he listened, really listened, for some kind of meaning in the tune of the gale. The in and exhale of the gusts resembled a sound that reminded him of how Paige breathed when she fell into a deep, tranquil sleep. The way she slept before she got sick. He thought about crying but didn't. Just sat there for a while, listening to Wyoming breathe. Painless. Un-wincing. Breathing with the peace she always had and always would, and maybe he wasn't so sick of her song after all. Getting to his feet, Luke brushed the snow off his Carhartts, prayed for a little fortitude and looked ahead. A small gold-something was glinting in the snow a hundred yards off in the direction of the house. He walked toward the glint, his ankle beginning to throb again, but he remembered his prayer and kept his poise. All Luke could do was stick to the fundamentals and win today. That's all anyone could do. Just chew on their problems one small, manageable bite at a time until their daily bread was eaten. Just try to leave the world a little better place when he got into bed than it was when he got out of it.

This was the code of the West—the cowboy way.

Reaching down, he picked up the glinting-something—an empty can of Copenhagen chewing tobacco. The lid made of aluminum and painted faux gold. It had probably blown over from the road after his neighbor Bill Morris chucked it out the window of his truck on Alden Keller's road. Luke hated littering. His typical day out in the pastures always took about ten minutes longer than it should've because he was always stopping the truck on his way home to pick up the beer can someone had littered from the highway. Sometimes he wished he was one of those people who could just drive by trash besmirching his land and not feel a sense of duty to get out and pick it up. The first thing he wanted to do when he got home was call Bill and rip him a new one he'd never forget about how Luke was tired of always picking up his beer and chew cans on his property, always being the one to mend their shared fences every spring…then he remembered how Paige had loved Bill. Had always said deep down he was a good man who was prone to make poor choices. Had always seen the best in him and tried her best to help him see it too. Even sent him letters once a month when he went to prison for a year. Bill had responded to that, had come to Paige's funeral and spoke to Luke for a good five minutes about how much he admired his wife and how broken up he was about her death.

Unbuttoning the breast pocket of his Carhartt, Luke dropped the can in and continued his walk, thinking of tangible ways to win the day. He'd go in the house for a few minutes and warm up, then get the tractor and pull the truck out. He wouldn't take the shortcut in the snow anymore. He'd take the long way next time and not get stuck. Whenever he finally finished feeding, he'd attempt to make the girls chicken tortilla casserole for dinner.

Then, sometime in the next week, he'd buy a plane ticket to Kenya. Over the last month, he'd been debating whether or not to take the trip. Not by anyone's suggestion—he'd just always wanted to go to Africa and, for some reason, remembered Paige showing him a picture in *National Geographic* of a hot air balloon drifting over the Maasai Mara National Reserve. Practical reasons not to take the trip had so far hindered him from pulling the trigger—cost, time off, what to do with the girls, the absolute necessity of going—but at this point, he felt convicted he wasn't abusing the phrase *I need a vacation*.

For his sake and the girls', he really did.

It had felt appropriate to dwell in the darkness since he'd lost Paige that late December day. To fight grief's initial surge would be to deny his humanity. He recognized it would be a long time before he finished grieving her, but he also knew it was time to start coming out of the darkness. To see the sun shine down on a part of the Earth he'd never seen, a place un-haunted by the painful memories stalking every acre of his usual, beloved scenery.

The time had come when sorrow was asking Luke to stay with her forever. Deranged as it seemed, she looked very beautiful in this moment. The violin under her quivering chin as she fervently worked the bow over the string to cry out her cold and beautiful melody. Her cheeks, red and tear-streaked, begging to be kissed. Luke felt her trying to wrap him in her arms forever and knew if he didn't go to Kenya, he'd end up in her embrace for the rest of his life. Exhausted, he clambered up the porch steps and saw a drab green Pyrex dish covered with tinfoil sitting in front of the door, a large yellow Post-it note stuck on top—

Paige always told me how much you and the girls loved this. Mine isn't as good, but hopefully it brings a little comfort during a hard time. Don't forget about the grief support group tonight. I think it will help. Amy said she could watch the girls. –Grace.

CHAPTER 22

The Windy City and State

March 6, 1992—Cheyenne, WY ||

They couldn't have picked a more depressing basement to hold a grief support group.

Luke thought as he contemplated the most colorless room he'd ever seen. The lights fluorescent and harsh, the walls pale and lifeless, the linoleum floor ash gray and freezing. He wished he was home with the girls, eating chicken tortilla casserole.

His fellow grievers were also depressing. He didn't fit in with their kind of grief. Their kind of grief was the sad kind. His, the tragic. His kind of grief had forgotten homework and three hundred cattle to feed. Their kind had fake hips and hearing aids. His got stuck in the snow. Theirs remembered the time…

"We'd only been married for about a year. George lived in Wyoming all his life, but I grew up in the Midwest," a woman named Ethel said with a wistful smile. "We couldn't afford plane tickets, so we drove to Chicago for the holidays to see my folks. We were trying to make it back to Cheyenne that night. It was three in the morning—snowing and blowing so hard you couldn't tell the difference between a cow and a cowboy. And lemme tell you, the blizzard of '49 was the worst I'd ever seen. We ran off the road and got stuck in a drift the size of Texas. Didn't have chains, didn't have a shovel, and we were seven miles from Cheyenne. So all we could do was stay in the truck and keep each other warm till morning. I thought I was going to freeze to death, so George, uh, got the blood flowing to my extremities again, if you know what I mean…"

She looked at Luke and winked, and before he could blush, his ears harked a tone of joviality.

"Ha!" A perfect and beautiful laugh rang out somewhere behind him. He turned around, and standing at the door were hips and dark curly hair and cold hands holding the most delicious-looking tray of cream puffs he'd ever seen. Whoever she was, she was incredibly late, but nevertheless, there she stood.

"And after I could feel my hands again, it was still too cold to sleep. So we just talked about snow all night. How it's all cold and beautiful, and how a lot of people had talked about how it's cold. And a lot of people had talked about how it's beautiful. But we wondered if we were the first people in the world to talk about how it was both of those things all at once. And we imagined that everyone wanted that. Wanted to be the first people in the world to think of something. How we all just want to be snowflakes—all unique and splendid and falling with grace. But when you really think about it, a snowflake isn't snow. It takes a whole bunch of flakes to be called snow. It's weird that we call *them* snowflakes but call *it* snow. And it makes you feel cold and beautiful to think how everyone wants to be a snowflake. And everyone wants to be snow. And is there any way to be both those things at once? We waxed all philosophic like that till the sun came up…and I know it wasn't the most beautiful sunrise I'd ever seen because, well, you couldn't really see it with that all-encompassing snow cloud blanketing it from sight, but in that moment I decided to claim it was."

CHAPTER 23

The Dress Aquatic

August 28, 1992—Cheyenne, WY

Diana didn't know what to wear.

He was really handsome—rugged, yet still refined. Simple but sophisticated and not ignorant. A kind of Renaissance rancher. She was finally going on a date with Luke Bainbridge. After they'd met at the grief support group, he'd taken a much-needed vacation to Kenya. Shortly after he got back, Diana had taken the boys on a long road trip across the country to see family and friends.

"I just want him to like me," she told herself in the bathroom mirror almost six months after they'd met.

"Who do you want to like you?" Jeremy boomed, tearing open the shower curtain.

"Gaaa!" Diana screamed.

"Yeah Mom! Who is 'him?'" Mick joined.

"Yeah Ma! Who 'him?'" Charlie followed. He looked up at his bosses to see if he'd done his job. Jeremy glanced at him, winked, then turned his focus back to their mother, Mick and Charlie following suit.

"Work party huh?" Jeremy said skeptically.

"Boys...just—"

"What?"

"I'm sorry I lied to you. It's just, well, I have a date, and I didn't know how you'd feel about it. Your father's only been gone for a year, and I…"

"You're waiting for him to get more dead?" Jeremy smiled.

"Yeah Mom. Maybe if you wait another year, he'll be even deader," Mick joined.

"Ha! Yah. Dead-dead!" Charlie finished.

"Well, what do you think I should wear?" she said, taking off her third outfit.

"Dat wan!" Charlie pointed candidly to an aqua dress—the most colorful thing in the closet he could find. Like his mother, he loved bright colors.

"Char, I can't wear tha—" He started crying. She sighed, grabbed it off the hanger, slipped it on and looked in the mirror again. Charlie looked at Jeremy and smiled. Like all good Westermans, her boys had a gift for persuasion.

"This doesn't hide my hips…"

"I think you look really beautiful Mom," Mick said, then added, "He will too."

"Yeah," Jeremy shrugged. "And if he doesn't, we'll kill him."

She decided to stick with the aqua dress.

#

She looked radiant.

Brazenly elegant and easy on the eyes, the aqua dress was tailored perfectly for her figure. Nobody pulled off an aqua dress quite like Diana. A beautiful Armenian woman with a big beating heart, soft mocha skin, and strong hips.

Most women would kill for her décolletage. Her swirling, dark chocolate hair paired with her hazel eyes like dessert and coffee. Her mocha-dark tones and features, accented by the radiance of the aqua dress…well, it was over for Luke Bainbridge the moment she opened the door to leave for their date. He took her to Applebee's, which in Cheyenne was one of the fancier joints for a first date. She ordered the artichoke dip. He got the steak fajitas. Like many of the scenes in this story, the narrator can only imagine the actual conversation that transpired in that small sliver of time and space.

But he imagines they talk about God's faithfulness. He imagines they talk about the deaths of their first loves and the Great War both their fathers fought on the respective beaches of the Atlantic and Pacific. He imagines the romance and poetry of that night felt very tangible and practical as they left the restaurant and drove back to the house he was sleeping in, sharing their cold and beautiful stories with each other on the back porch till midnight…

CHAPTER 24

Where Heaven Meets Cheyenne

September 5, 1992–Cheyenne, WY

Charlie was actually there for their second date (sort of). It was...well, not really much of a date at all. Luke called her the next day as promised, and she was so excited to see him again that—had he asked—she probably would've joined him for a tour of a mortuary. Instead, she extended him an invitation to the circus before she even realized the words were coming out of her mouth.

"It's my son Mick's sixth birthday on Saturday. Would you and your girls like to join us for enchiladas and cake at the house?"

And Charlie was sort of there for it. He was just shy of two and a half years old the first time he met his first real cowboy, so his memories of that night are contained in small, vivid flashes. He doesn't remember them coming in the door and being formally introduced, but he remembers being the youngest of five kids sitting around a little round brown table and eating enchiladas, looking up and seeing his mother and the cowboy at the dining room table smiling at each other a lot, and it made him like the cowboy. He liked the cowboy's daughters too. They were nice to him and had lost their mom, just like he and his brothers had lost their dad.

Believe it or not, he can recall a lot of stuff before that night.

Ever since he can remember, he remembers understanding two things. One—that his father died. And two—that when he died, he went to Heaven and was watching over him. But he doesn't remember anyone ever sitting him down and explaining all that. Maybe they did, but all he knows is that this knowledge has always felt engrained in the understanding of his existence, which has always given his existence the feeling of an invisible hand on his shoulder. Something guiding him down a path leading somewhere meaningful. He remembers this hand nudging him awake in the middle of the night a lot after his father died. He'd climb out of bed, and the hand would guide him to the foot of his toy shelf, which at the time seemed like a great ladder to some grand, far-off place. He'd climb till his feet were on the third row of shelves, then levitate on his tiptoes to see the stars and city lights shining through the window. And he'd look out at Heaven and Cheyenne and try to figure out where one ended and the other began. They all looked like stars to him. His eyes wandering from one star to the next, trying to figure out which one Chuck Westerman was watching him from…

So yes. He remembers glimpses of Mick's sixth birthday/Luke and Diana's (sort of) second date. The little round brown table and enchiladas. The colored balloons tied to the back of the chairs. Haley, Jeremy, Emma and himself all with one each, but since he was the birthday boy, Mick got a whole rainbow of balloons to himself. Then it all went to pot when Emma had the audacity to show her admiration for their beauty by touching them, which caused Mick to get so angry he ran upstairs to his room screaming—and remember, Charlie was two and a half when this happened, so his memory of this moment might not be entirely accurate—but Charlie is pretty sure he screamed something like, "What I'm really angry about is the fact that my little brother is so much better looking and smarter than me!"

Or something to that effect.

Moments later, Mick came out of his room bear-hugging a zoo full of stuffed animals, set them on the ground next to him like cannon balls, and started firing them one at a time down the stairs, Diana's face buried so deep in her palms Charlie couldn't tell, but he imagines it matched the red balloon on the back of the birthday boy's chair.

CHAPTER 25

Twenty Years in Twenty Seconds

September 11, 1992—Cheyenne, WY

Luke suspected Mick wasn't really angry about the balloons.

He got the sense that behind his impressive outburst was a six-year-old's fear of growing up without a father. To Diana's surprise, he called again a few days later and asked if she'd be interested in going on date number three.

She'd love to.

He took her to see *Wind*, starring Matthew Modine and Jennifer Grey. Neither of them could recollect much of the storyline. Something about yacht racing and falling in love, maybe? Who cared. They had more important things on their mind, like falling in love again in real life. Somewhere in the third act, Luke noticed Diana's hand dubiously placed for him to take on the armrest. It looked cold. He took his right hand and slid it gently under, then used his other hand to cloak the top of hers.

Time stopped and flew all at once. The rest of the movie lasting twenty years and twenty seconds. They saw it all—a rainbow-themed wedding signifying God's faithfulness to Noah after the flood. A 1,400-acre yard. One Diana's wild sons would finally deem big enough to play in. The two beautiful daughters she'd never had. A popup camper hitched to a green seven-passenger van roaming across the West from national park to national park on annual summer vacations. A big dining room table hosting lively conversation, seven plates heaped with meat and potatoes, that nice grainy bread that nourishes strong bones. A piano in the den. A hoop in the driveway. A small town to grow up in and a large map of the world hanging above the breakfast table in the kitchen, a reminder that people also live in big cities.

Roll credits.

Some in the theater lingered to check out the cast, but by the time they got to the "Rude Lady on Yacht" character, everyone was gone. Everyone except Luke and Diana. They just sat there, holding hands. Pondering the same overwhelming but important thought—look at all these names, all these long and complex stories we'll never know past "Peter La Chouffe, Assistant Special Effects Coordinator."

Someone could've asked them, "Tell me the story of Peter La Chouffe," and they'd have replied, "Well, he was the Assistant Special Effects Coordinator for the movie *Wind*." But that didn't even begin to tell the story of Peter La Chouffe. They'd never know that when Peter graduated high school, he went to Cleveland with his dad and accidentally found a letter in his briefcase from a woman that wasn't his mother. That this is what drove Peter to volunteer for poverty through college and his twenties. What gave him the resolve to work his tail off till he got paid to do something where his own hands had the power to change how a story was told. *That* Peter, the real Peter, they'd never know. And they'd never know the real Donna Rodriguez, assistant to Ms. Grey. And what did they know of stunt boat driver Jack

Benny? Other than his thrill for testing the patience of physics and that he probably had to say, "Yes, like the comedian," nine times out of ten times he introduced himself to someone.

Finally, there was no more credit due. Every name and story that came together to create the story of *Wind* had been inadequately acknowledged.

"Do you like walks?" Diana asked.

"It's my favorite mode of transportation."

"I know it's getting late, but what do you think about going for a late-night walk in the park?"

"I think that's one of the best ideas I've heard in a while."

They walked in Lion's Park, holding hands and grazing shoulders. "So what do you think about wind?" Luke asked.

"Oh…it was, well, to be honest, I really wasn't paying much attention."

"Not the movie, the element. You know, the great unseen force?"

"Ohhh…*wind*-wind."

"Yes, wind-wind."

"I'll say this—it's not easy having *this* hair in *this* state, I'll tell you that." Luke smiled. "What about you? You grew up here. You must have some thoughts about wind."

He didn't say anything for about a minute. Just stared ahead with a look of organizing thoughts and the careful choosing of words to articulate them.

"I couldn't live the life I do without it. We get just enough moisture around here to grow enough grass and provide the cattle with food, but not enough to form a natural water supply. The mills we built furnish that, but they're not very effective without—you guessed it—*wind*. Like about everything in life, it's a tradeoff. I don't exactly love it in January when

I have to feed cattle in it, but I'm sure happy for a breeze to turn the mills when it's a hundred degrees on the Fourth of July. When you've got fourteen hundred cattle who need seven to ten gallons a day to survive in the summer, you're in an awfully tough spot if it doesn't blow for a week. The way I see it, if we had less wind, I wouldn't be able to live here and do what I do and have the good life I have."

It's funny, isn't it?

Wind. Always reminding us there are things we can't see or control no matter how hard we try. Pressing that humbling thought into our minds we try to push away…

The only thing you really control is your soul. Everything else will someday turn to dust and blow away, and only one question will remain—what did you do with the only thing you could?

ACKNOWLEDGMENTS

It's been a twelve year journey finally getting this sucker in print. Let's just say it was bit of a delicate book to write. I can't quite remember who first loaned me the phrase "autobiographical fiction," but my first debt of gratitude goes out to them for giving me a liberating yet defined approach to the writing of it. Calling it that, I felt, gave me the appropriate grace to tell the story as I saw artistically and emotionally fit while also, I hope, not imposing my perception of the painful, but in the end, beautiful, events that prompted my telling of it as the ultimate say for how it all transpired. For that, I would like to thank everyone who is familiar with and close to the real life story for the encouragement or, at the very least, tolerance they have afforded me to spin this yarn my way.

Plenty of people don't have the fortune of having one amazing parent in their life to guide them through it. For whatever reason, I was blessed with three, and I can't even begin to describe how thankful I am for that guiding presence, especially as I tried to tell their story. On Earth and in Heaven, you have played crucial roles in my development as a writer and a person. To my oldest brother Jeremy, whatever confidence and identity I have in putting the man in Westerman, I owe to you. To my next oldest brother Mick, whatever confidence and identity I have in being a writer, you have "brothered" that like no one else in my life. Abby and Hannah, I couldn't ask for better sisters, and know you've had more impact on my creative growth and cultural enlightenment than you probably realize. I'm also grateful for my awesome in-laws Tara, Stef, Tom and Ben.

    Writing is a lonely game. Luckily, outside of my immediate family, I've been blessed with people who have been instrumental in my writing journey and made it less lonely. I don't have room here to thank all the friends and family who have been individually supportive of this book at different points in its process, but know that if you have, it was deeply appreciated. In particular, I want to thank Brendon Mount, who I've grown up with creatively since we moved to Portland together after college and is one of the greatest American songwriters of my generation most people don't know about. Seriously, check out The Doubt's newest album, *It's All A Joke*, on Spotify. Matt, Travis, Danny, Luke, Madi, TJ, Max, Ben and Eric all come to mind when I think of my inner circle of support during that trivial and transformative period of life known as the early twenties. Thank you to Ella Snow for being the first person in the book world to really believe this was a story worth telling. Your feedback and encouragement were crucial. Shoutout to all the people at Atmosphere Press who helped finally get this story in print and reach its highest potential. You've been great to work with. To all the incredible teachers and professors I had who taught me about writing and literature, I truly can't thank you enough.

    To Whitney—you are the love of my friggin' life. It took awhile for us to find each other, but I've read somewhere that the best boo thangs in life take time.

    I hate a shameless plug as much as anyone, but most people get a steady paycheck for good hard work in their field. Many in the creative fields never yield the financial fruits of their labors. If you read this book and enjoyed it, please passionately tell your friends about it, give it to your crazy uncle for his birthday, put it in your mother's stocking at Christmas, sing its praises from the virtual mountaintops of your various social media platforms…you get the idea. If I could make a high school English teacher's annual salary off this story, it would make a serious difference for a young family trying to find their footing in the increasingly shifty economic times we're all trying to navigate these days.

ABOUT ATMOSPHERE PRESS

Founded in 2015, Atmosphere Press was built on the principles of Honesty, Transparency, Professionalism, Kindness, and Making Your Book Awesome. As an ethical and author-friendly hybrid press, we stay true to that founding mission today.

If you're a reader, enter our giveaway for a free book here:

SCAN TO ENTER
BOOK GIVEAWAY

If you're a writer, submit your manuscript for consideration here:

SCAN TO SUBMIT
MANUSCRIPT

And always feel free to visit Atmosphere Press and our authors online at atmospherepress.com. See you there soon!

ABOUT THE AUTHOR

CHARLES MACDUFF WESTERMAN grew up on a cattle ranch in Chugwater, Wyoming. He graduated from Washington State University with a degree in Journalism and English Literature in May of 2012. After college, he moved to Portland, Oregon, working as a school bus driver and writing *Where Heaven Meets Cheyenne* at coffee shops between his morning and afternoon routes. In 2020, he completed *The Book Project* with Lighthouse Writers in Denver, Colorado, where he currently resides. These days, he teaches high school English and coaches boys basketball and just might even be married by the time this book finally comes out.

Follow on Instagram: charles.macduff
Follow on X: @cmwesterman